Community and Responsibility in the Jewish Tradition

Revised Edition

Barbara Steinberg

Updated and Revised by Dara Gabrielle Zabb

Edited by Karen L. Stein

A STUDY AND ACTION PROGRAM

United Synagogue of Conservative Judaism
Department of Youth Activities

Production Editor: Ari Y. Goldberg

A publication of the National Youth Commission,
United Synagogue of Conservative Judaism
155 Fifth Avenue, New York, New York 10010

http://www.uscj.org/usy

Revised Edition, 1999

Manufactured in the United States of America

TABLE OF CONTENTS

GUIDE TO HEBREW NAMES FOR BOOKS OF THE BIBLE

Bereshit = Genesis

Shemot = Exodus

Vayikra = Leviticus

Bamidbar = Numbers

Devarim = Deuteronomy

Shoftim = Judges

Melakhim = Kings

Tehillim = Psalms

Mishlei = Proverbs

Shir HaShirim = Song of Songs

Eicha = Lamentations

Kohelet = Ecclesiastes

≈ EDITOR'S PREFACE TO REVISED EDITION ≈

Over 20 years ago, USY published a sourcebook that was considered for years to be an invaluable resource for Jewish educators. ***Tzorchei Tzibbur: Community and Responsibility in the Jewish Tradition*** has been utilized in Hebrew High Schools across North America, studied by countless USYers in study groups in their regions and cited by numerous other publications, web sites and Jewish education resources. It has been widely acclaimed by Rabbis and educators for its comprehensive inclusion of traditional textual sources as well as how it relates to modern concerns.

Now, as we reach the end of the 20th century, ***Tzorchei Tzibbur*** has been revised and updated but still maintains its timeless value. The primary difference between the two editions of ***Tzorchei Tzibbur*** is the inclusion of explanations and exercises in the new text. In 1978, a parallel teacher's guide was developed to accompany the student text. This newly revised edition was designed to allow the independent learner to work through the book without necessarily needing an instructor.

We are very grateful to the talented group of readers who played a crucial role in shaping this book:

Sarrae Crane
Rabbi Jerome M. Epstein
Marsha Goldwasser
Jonathan S. Greenberg
Jack Gruenberg
Jules A. Gutin
Ze'ev Kainan
David Srebnik
Barbara Steinberg
Rabbi Charles Savenor
Gila Hadani Ward

I must also extend my deepest appreciation to Dara Zabb who constantly strove to create a text that would appeal first and foremost to teenagers. I am grateful to Ari Goldberg, the revised edition's Production Editor, who is my *Rav* (my teacher) and my *Haver* (my friend). The third floor staff of the Youth Department of the United Synagogue of Conservative Judaism have all been extremely supportive throughout the entire revision process, particularly Jules Gutin and Gila Hadani Ward for all of their comments and assistance in guiding the overall project, and Ze'ev Kainan whose suggestions for the Pidyon Shevuyim chapter were instrumental in shaping and focusing the chapter. Additionally, thank you to Dana Stein for helping to bring the original manuscript into the 21st century—by typing it into a PC.

In the 16th century, Rabbi Isaac Luria commented that in his world—much like in ours—many things seemed to be wrong. People suffered from hunger, disease, hatred, and war. "How could God allow such terrible things to happen?" wondered Luria. "Perhaps," he suggested, "it is because God needs our help." As Conservative Jews, we recognize the importance of taking action and helping to build a better world through mitzvot and the love for our neighbors. It is for this reason that we read ***Tzorchei Tzibbur: Community and Responsibility in the Jewish Tradition.***

Karen L. Stein
November 1999

≈ EDITOR'S PREFACE TO FIRST EDITION ≈

This sourcebook, *Tzorchei Tzibbur: Community and Responsibility* in the Jewish tradition, is not yet complete. You—in your studies and action projects—will be completing it by workbook activities and community program involvement. As with no other USY sourcebook, this publication is geared primarily for use in groups (i.e., communities) with the companion *Advisor's/Teacher's Edition*, although an individual reading through the book may well derive benefit from it.

United Synagogue Youth is very grateful to Barbara Fortgang Summers, who has devoted much time and effort creating, researching, and writing this volume, as well as planning and testing the instructional guidelines of the *Advisor's/Teacher's Edition*. She has combined the best of formal and informal Jewish educational methods. The original manuscript also benefited from the reactions and advice of individuals whom we thank for their time and guidance: Muriel Bermar, Bruce Greenfield, Jules Gutin, Karen Legman Segal, Alan Teperow, and Rabbis Joel Epstein, Paul Freedman, Neil Gillman, Marvin Goodman, Neal Kaunfer, and Barry Dov Lerner. Their contribution to the success of this project—as well as the resource information of many other individuals—is acknowledged with gratitude.

As you read through the source material, you will notice that various mitzvoth are not introduced by b'rachot (blessings). Unlike most aspects of Jewish life, the acts we will study here have no accompanying b'rachot, since (as Professor Max Kadushin explains) the actions themselves embody the purpose of the blessing. (Besides that, can you imagine what b'rachah one would recite upon giving tzedakah or fulfilling any of the other mitzvot we will examine!)

The mitzvot which comprise "the needs of the community" are matters of social responsibility and religious *obligation*, no less part of Jewish law than Shabbat or Kashrut. We present them as projects each of us can adopt and encourage for even more than values to protest *against*, the Jewish tradition affords us causes to protest *for*, fulfilling our communal responsibility.

S.G.

≈ PREFACE TO REVISED EDITION ≈

The sage Hillel said: *In a place where there are no humans, we must strive to be human.*

I learned the value of community responsibility from my father, who, in his entire career working for the Human Resources Administration of New York City, always thought of the people that he helped as nothing less than human beings.

The essence of ***Tzorchei Tzibbur: Community and Responsibility in the Jewish Tradition*** is rooted in the moral and ethical code of Judaism that demands that as human beings, we must be responsible for each other. We continue to thrive as a Jewish community because we recognize that one of our most sacred gifts as human beings is that we are here, together, in order to influence and help each other.

But the task is not simple. We live in a world where the beauty of our rich tradition is closely surrounded by poverty, violence, and discrimination. It is our job to draw strength from this tradition, and to resist conceding to, or being apathetic towards an issue that we might perceive as somebody else's problem.

It is my hope that this sourcebook will serve as the impetus for Jewish students of all ages to take responsibility for the world that we live in. Moreover, I hope that this sourcebook will serve to increase our own understanding of how the relationship between Judaism and community responsibility is truly singular.

Barbara Steinberg provided me with a first edition replete with sacred sources that were invaluable in crafting the updated version of her original text. It is her acute vision of ***Tzorchei Tzibbur*** that provided the backbone for this project.

I want to thank the staff of the United Synagogue Youth for their support and guidance during this process, especially to Karen Stein, Editor of this sourcebook, and my *hevruta* for this project.

I would be remiss if I didn't thank my parents, family, friends and teachers at the Jewish Theological Seminary for their unwavering patience during this endeavor.

Dara Gabrielle Zabb
Kislev 5760

≈ PREFACE TO FIRST EDITION ≈

A number of people helped me to write *Tzorchei Tzibbur* and I want to thank them for their advice and for the time they have devoted to this project.

Ms. Annette Avner, Mrs. Sylvia Avner, and Ms. Donna Fishman spent long summer days and nights listening to my thoughts and challenging them, improving my plans with their ideas.

Dr. Joel Roth and Dr. Ephraim Shimoff helped in locating rabbinic sources and in clarifying the concepts they teach.

Mr. Samuel Steinberg helped me to define the goals of the educational activities and to focus on the sensitivities and needs of the students who will participate in the activities.

Rabbis Stephen Garfinkel and Robert Summers have been closely associated with the development of the *Tzorchei Tzibbur* program. Steve initiated the project, and his efforts have made the publication of this program possible. Robbie encouraged me to accept the invitation to write *Tzorchei Tzibbur* and continued to encourage me in many ways throughout the time I worked on the project.

Finally, the Jewish families whom I visited in the Soviet Union during June 1978, served as a constant source of inspiration for me.

There is no simple way for me to thank all of these people. If the *Tzorchei Tzibbur* program succeeds in influencing young Jews to take pride in Jewish values and act upon them, the success will be due in large part to the dedication to these values of the people I have mentioned above.

Barbara Fortgang Summers
November 1978

≈ INTRODUCTION ≈

Tzorchei Tzibbur: Community and Responsibility in the Jewish Tradition is a source and activity book designed to combine study and action. Rabbi Tarfon and the sages gathered together late one night and argued over which is greater: *midrash* (study of Torah) or *ma'aseh* (actions of good deeds). Rabbi Tarfon answered that the performance of good deeds was more important. Rabbi Akiva answered that the study of Torah was more valuable. Finally, the Rabbis determined that study is preferable to action only inasmuch as study leads to greater involvement in performing mitzvot. *Tzorchei Tzibbur* is based on this rabbinic premise and on the notion that the best way to teach people how to do something is to do it.

BEFORE WE BEGIN

The traditional sources are used in a number of ways: often they confront or encourage feelings; frequently they introduce new ideas and attitudes toward communal responsibility. On some occasions, the sources are presented with information about their historical origins and background; on others, they stand as timeless indicators of Jewish attitudes and values. The sources are seen as a means to two ends: as they are provocative and inspirational, they may spur actions; as they represent problems that face us today, they link together Jewish generations of the past and present.

FYI
Hevruta, which stems from the Hebrew word HAVER, meaning friend, is a great way to learn Jewish texts. *Hevrutot* (plural for *hevruta*) are small study groups where you can talk about the meaning of the texts, ask provocative and informed questions and learn from each other. Setting up a *hevruta* for each topic in this sourcebook is a great educational tool.

HOW TO MAKE THE MOST OUT OF THE JEWISH SOURCES

Throughout *Tzorchei Tzibbur*, traditional sources are quoted in an attempt to use the past to help to plan for the future. You may choose to work with texts you find especially appealing, incorporate additional textual references, or find other material on your own. Generally, the primary sources are provided for the values they embody.

TZORCHEI TZIBBUR AND THE JEWISH PEOPLE

You may wonder: What is Jewish about visiting the sick, offering hospitality, or comforting mourners? *Tzorchei Tzibbur* utilizes traditional texts to respond to this question: tzedakah and gemilut hasadim (acts of lovingkindness) are deeply rooted in the character of the Jewish people. Furthermore, showing concern for the needs of others—and for one's own needs—is a mitzvah, a standard of behavior that guides Jews in their relationships with each other and with the rest of the world. Although our "copyright" on these sensitive behaviors has expired, nevertheless, we as Jews bring some special concerns to community services.

We support the poor through a system of self-taxation. We extend gemilut hasadim beyond the sphere of our friends and acquaintances: we welcome strangers into our communities and homes; we even visit people we do not know when they are ill; we ransom captives even if we have no previous experience with them personally. Simply knowing that others are in need, forces the Jewish people to act on their behalf. Furthermore, no other people have developed so comprehensive a body of legislation for dealing with the sensitivity of individual and community toward those in need. Judaism legislates—*requires, demands*—of Jews what others may *choose* to do. These qualifications of the Jewish involvement in serving our fellows do not make us better or worse than other people. They make us different and form a unique aspect of our identity as a Jewish People. Most simply put, THEY MAKE US JEWS.

WHAT MAKES US RESPONSIBLE?

In order to define "Community and Responsibility in the Jewish Tradition," we need to first define which community or communities we are responsible for. As Jews, we show concern for our own community. Does that mean that we are only responsible for our own community? Should we make ourselves responsible to other communities?

➤ How can we determine whether or not Judaism espouses our being responsible for issues that are not intrinsic to our own community?

Exercise: What Makes an Issue Jewish?

Below is a list of current local and international community issues. Are these issues that the Jewish community should be concerned with? Why or why not? Think about what makes an issue 'Jewish.'

	YES/NO	REASON
Abortion		
AIDS		
Crime Prevention		
Disease Prevention and Cures		
Environment		
Equal Rights (women, minorities)		
Global Warming		
Gun Control		
Health Care Reform		
Immigration Reform		
Peace in The Middle East		
Safety in Public Schools		
Saving the Whales		
Welfare Reform		

➤ On what did you base your decisions?

You may have based your decision on the Jewish values written in Torah that have been passed down from generation to generation. Take a look at some of the textual sources that follow and see if any of them concur with your reasoning.

Judaism dictates that we are responsible not only for our own community, but for other communities as well.

➢ How do we know this?

LOVE YOUR NEIGHBOR AS YOURSELF וְאָהַבְתָּ לְרֵעֲךָ כָּמוֹךָ

➢ What does *v'ahavta l'recha kamocha,* "love your neighbor as yourself," mean to you?

Judaism provides an inclusive definition of *v'ahavta l'recha kamocha:*

לֹא־תִשְׂנָא אֶת־אָחִיךָ בִּלְבָבֶךָ הוֹכֵחַ תּוֹכִיחַ אֶת־עֲמִיתֶךָ וְלֹא־תִשָּׂא עָלָיו חֵטְא׃
לֹא־תִקֹּם וְלֹא־תִטֹּר אֶת־בְּנֵי עַמֶּךָ וְאָהַבְתָּ לְרֵעֲךָ כָּמוֹךָ אֲנִי יְהוָה׃

You shall not hate your kinsman in your heart. Reprove your neighbor, but incur no guilt because of him. You shall not take vengeance or bear a grudge against your kinsfolk. Love your neighbor as yourself: I am the Lord. Vayikra 19:17-18

וְכִי־יָגוּר אִתְּךָ גֵּר בְּאַרְצְכֶם לֹא תוֹנוּ אֹתוֹ׃ כְּאֶזְרָח מִכֶּם יִהְיֶה לָכֶם הַגֵּר ׀ הַגָּר
אִתְּכֶם וְאָהַבְתָּ לוֹ כָּמוֹךָ כִּי־גֵרִים הֱיִיתֶם בְּאֶרֶץ מִצְרָיִם אֲנִי יְהוָה אֱלֹהֵיכֶם׃

When a stranger resides with you in your land, you shall not wrong him. The stranger who resides with you shall be to you as one of your citizens; you shall love him as yourself, for you were strangers in the land of Egypt: I am the Lord your God. Vayikra 19: 33-34

We see that the Rabbis of Talmudic times recognized the importance of these concepts through the stories they tell:

שוב מעשה בנכרי אחד שבא לפני שמאי, אמר לו: גיירני על מנת שתלמדני
כל התורה כולה כשאני עומד על רגל אחת. דחפו באמת הבנין שבידו. בא
לפני הלל, גייריה. אמר לו: דעלך סני לחברך לא תעביד - זו היא כל
התורה כולה, ואידך - פירושה הוא.

There is a story told of a man who wanted to learn everything about the Torah. The man went up to Rabbi Shammai and said, "Can you teach me the Torah while I stand on one foot?" Rabbi Shammai looked at him and laughed. "You crazy fool! I can not teach you the entire Torah in such a short of time." The man walked away and soon came upon Rabbi Hillel. Again, he asked the same questions, "Can you teach me the Torah while I stand one foot?" Rabbi Hillel thought for just a moment and then replied, "What is hateful to you, do not do unto your neighbor. This is the entire Torah; all the rest is commentary." Shabbat 31a

THE TRUTH ABOUT TZEDAKAH AND GEMILUT HASADIM

A story is told of three people who go down to the end of a river to find that there are dead fish floating in the water. The first person shakes his head, put his hands behind his back and walks away. The second person wades into the water and starts to pull out the fish one by one, and the third person walks up to the mouth of the river to find out why all these fish are ending up dead at the end of the river.

- ➢ **How would you label the kind of 'action' that each person took in the story?**
- ➢ **What are the differences/similarities between the actions that each person took?**
- ➢ **How could we define the people's actions in the story with Jewish terms?**

Using the definitions for Gemilut Hasadim and Tzedakah that appear below, which person in the story represents Tzedakah and which person represents Gemilut Hasadim? Why?

We often use the words Tzedakah and Gemilut Hasadim interchangeably. However, each one has its own distinct definition. In order to understand Community Responsibility from a Jewish perspective, we must first understand the difference between Tzedakah and Gemilut Hasadim.

TZEDAKAH

צדקה - בממונו, גמילות חסדים - בין בגופו בין בממונו. צדקה - לעניים, גמילות חסדים - בין לעניים בין לעשירים. צדקה - לחיים, גמילות חסדים - בין לחיים בין למתים.

Tzedakah can be given only with one's money; Gemilut Hasadim, both by personal service and with money.

Tzedakah can be given only to the poor; Gemilut Hasadim, both to the rich and the poor.

Tzedakah can be given only to the living; Gemilut Hasadim, both to the living and the dead.
Sukkah 49b

The word *charity* is derived from a Latin root that means *love, natural affection, benevolence, or kindness.* The word *tzedakah* is derived from a Hebrew root that means *righteousness or justice.* That the Jewish people use the term *tzedakah* to label the action of giving money and physical sustenance to the poor shows a great deal about the attitude of Judaism toward this act. Jews perform acts of tzedakah not only because they want to, or because helping the poor is a fine thing to do. Jews do acts of tzedakah because helping to erase poverty and need in our fellows is the just and righteous thing to do. Tzedakah is prescribed by Jewish law in the same way that other social legislation was enacted in Biblical and Rabbinic law. Namely, to ensure justice between people and in order to guarantee that they do the right thing for one another.

GEMILUT HASADIM

גמילות חסדים: הדא דתימר בגופו אבל בממונו יש לו שיעור
ואתייא כיי דמר ר"ש בן לקיש בשם רבי יוסי בן חנינא באושא
נמנו שיהא אדם מפריש חומש מנכסיו למצוה.

Gemilut Hasadim can be expressed in personal service (with one's body) and with one's material goods. Only the former is unlimited in scope, whereas the latter is limited by the general rule that one should not distribute more than a fifth of one's possessions on good works. Jerusalem Talmud Pe'ah 2b

Gemilut Hasadim literally means "doing acts of loving kindness." In the Bible the word *hesed* means the love and loyalty that God shows for the Jewish people. When the rabbis in Talmudic times read the Torah, they found numerous expressions of God's love for the Jewish people. Most of these acts could only be done by God, but the rabbis felt some of them could be emulated by human beings. These acts of loving kindness that people can do for one another are known as *gemilut hasadim.* According to the rabbis, just as God clothed the naked (Adam and Eve in Bereshit 3:21), visited the sick (Abraham, an interpretation of Bereshit 18:1), comforted the mourners (Isaac in Bereshit 25:11), and buried the dead (Moses in Devarim 34:6), so too should the Jewish people perform these deeds, showing love to each other and to all mankind.

Exercise: Actions for the Community

You are about to study a number of community actions on behalf of those who are in need. Some of them are specifically acts of tzedakah, while others are part of the more inclusive category of gemilut hasadim. Below is a list of the topics discussed in this book. Which category do they belong in – tzedakah, gemilut hasadim, or both? Explain your decision!

	CATEGORY	WHY?
Giving money to the poor		
Visiting the sick		
Supporting a student through school		
Burying the dead		
Helping to save captives		
Showing hospitality to strangers/guests		
Respecting the elderly		
Dowering a bride		
Clothing the naked		
Feeding the hungry		

EXERCISE: Putting it in Your Own Words

- Write a definition for the mitzvah of tzedakah that would explain it to someone who does not know what it is:________________________________

____

____

____

____

- Write a definition for the mitzvah of gemilut hasadim that would explain it to someone who does not know what it means:________________________________

____

____

____

____

GETTING STARTED: TALKING ABOUT TZEDAKAH/GEMILUT HASADIM

There are six chapters in this sourcebook that examine topics at the forefront of concern within the Jewish community today. These topics include *Hachnasat Orchim* (hospitality), *Bikur Holim* (visiting the sick), *Hiddur P'nai Zaken* (respecting the aged), *Pidyon Shvuyim* (redeeming captives), *Kavod Hamet* (respect for the dead), and *Kavod He'ani* (respect for the poor).

Each chapter will help you to understand more about that particular issue. Included in each chapter are Jewish texts that correspond to that issue.

These topics are only the tip of the iceberg. Finding a community issue, which is of interest to you, is very important. Being passionate about the issue makes your hard work so much more rewarding. Unfortunately, there are so many different people and communities in this world that need our help. Sometimes, it can become overwhelming!

Just remember...

לא עליך המלאכה לגמור. ולא אתה בן חורין לבטל ממנה. (Avot 2:21)

Lo Alecha Hamlacha Ligmor—V'Lo atah Ben Chorin L'hivatel Mimenah.

You are not obligated to complete the task—neither are you free to ignore it.

EXERCISE: GETTING ORGANIZED

Choosing one or a few area(s) to become responsible for is not an easy process. This sourcebook is a great place to start! Here is a good litmus test to help you determine what you are passionate about:

In Menachot 43b, "Rabbi Meir says: Everyone must recite 100 Blessings each day."

A. Write down blessings that might be included in your daily 100 blessings.

B. If you attempt to ensure that other people could enjoy the same blessings that you think are important, how would you do it? Identify which of those actions on behalf of others would be acts of tzedakah and which would be gemilut hasadim?

1a.____

1b.____

____

2a.____

2b.____

____

3a.____

3b.____

____

4a.____

4b.____

____

Throughout the history of the Jewish people, Hachnasat Orchim (hospitality to guests) has been a standard of proper Jewish behavior. This mitzvah has developed into a means of showing personal and community concern for travelers and other guests. Our forefather Abraham exemplified hospitality to guests in the book of Bereshit (Genesis):

> *The Lord appeared to him [Abraham] by the terebinths of Mamre; he was sitting at the entrance of the tent as the day grew hot. Looking up, he saw three men standing near him. As soon as he saw them, he ran from the entrance of the tent to greet them and, bowing to the ground, he said, "My lords, if it please you, do not go on past your servant. Let a little water be brought; bathe your feet and recline under the tree. And let me fetch a morsel of bread that you may refresh yourselves; then go on – seeing that you have come your servant's way." They replied, "Do as you have said."*
>
> *Abraham hastened into the tent of Sarah, and said, "Quick, three measures of choice flour! Knead and make cakes!" Then Abraham ran to the herd, took a calf, tender and choice, and gave it to a servant-boy, who hastened to prepare it. He took curds and milk and the calf that had been prepared, and set these before them; and he waited on them under the tree as they ate.* *Bereshit 18:1-8*

TWO MITZVOT TOGETHER

Rabbinic tradition explains that one of the three messengers visited Abraham as an act of Bikur Holim (visiting the sick). The rabbis assume this visit to have taken place while Abraham was recuperating from his circumcision (Bereshit 17) since this chapter immediately follows the account of that part of Abraham's life. Nonetheless, Abraham's commitment to Hachnasat Orchim was so important to his well being, that God sent three angels in the guise of people, in order that Abraham be able to continue to welcome people even in his own time of need.

> **וירא אליו.** לבקר את החולה' אמר רבי חמא בר חנינא' יום שלישי למילתו היה' ובא הקב"ה ושאל בשלומו.
>
> ***And the Lord appeared to him.*** *To visit the sick man [Abraham]. Rabbi Hama the son of Hanina said: it was the third day after his circumcision and the Holy One, blessed be God's name, came and inquired about the state of his health.* Rashi on Bereshit 18:1

Warmly welcoming strangers and helping to satisfy their needs for food and lodging and for participation in religious celebrations grew to include friends and relatives, as well as wayfarers, to share in the joy of Shabbat and holiday meals. Hosting a guest for a Shabbat or a festival became a sign of status in Jewish communities around the world.

THE TALMUD ALSO TEACHES US AN IMPORTANT LESSON ABOUT HACHNASAT ORCHIM

זיל אייתי לי קמצא. אזל
אייתי ליה בר קמצא. אתא אשכחיה דהוה יתיב, אמר ליה: מכדי
ההוא גברא בעל דבבא דההוא גברא הוא, מאי בעית הכא? קום פוק
אמר ליה: הואיל ואתאי שבקן, ויהיבנא לך דמי מה דאכילנא ושתינא.
אמר ליה: לא. אמר ליה: יהיבנא לך דמי פלגא דסעודתיך. אמר ליה:
לא. אמר ליה: יהיבנא לך דמי כולה סעודתיך. א"ל: לא. נקטיה בידיה
ואוקמיה ואפקיה. אמר: הואיל והוו יתבי רבנן ולא מחו ביה, ש"מ קא
ניחא להו. איזיל איכול בהו קורצא בי מלכא. אזל אמר ליה לקיסר:
מרדו בך יהודאי.

A certain man had a friend Kamtza and an enemy Bar Kamtza. He once made a party and said to his servant, "Go and bring Kamtza." The servant went and (accidentally) brought Bar Kamtza to the party.

When the man [who gave the party] found him there he said, "See, you tell tales about me; what are you doing here? Get out." Said the other: "Since I am here, let me stay, and I will pay you for whatever I eat and drink." He said, "I won't." "Then let me give you half the cost of the party." "No," said the other. "Then let me pay for the whole party." He still said, "No," and he took him by the hand and put him out. Said the other "Since the Rabbis were sitting there and did not stop him, this shows that they agreed with him [the host]. I [Bar Kamtza] will go and inform against them to the government." He went and said to the Emperor. "The Jews are rebelling against you." Gittin 55b-56a

- Did something like this ever happen to you? How did you react?
- Why do you think Bar Kamtza came to the party? Didn't he know the host hated him?
- What is the best ending you could imagine for this story?
- What is the worst ending you could imagine for this story?

According to the text, the story concludes that ultimately, Jerusalem was destroyed because of Bar Kamtza's actions against the Jewish community vis a vis his behavior as a guest.

The story of Kamtza and Bar Kamtza becomes an important lesson for the Jewish community to pay attention to the importance of Hachnasat Orchim and how we treat our guests once they are in our homes.

FYI
The Talmud is made up of two components: the Mishnah, which is the first written summary of the Oral Law, and the Gemara (called Talmud in the more restricted sense of the term), which is formally an explanation and commentary on the Mishnah. In essence, the Talmud is a legal code that serves as a central pillar of support for Jewish law.

Hachnasat Orchim: A Personal Values Exercise

PART ONE: PERSONAL VALUES CONTINUA

Where do you stand on Hachnasat Orchim? Indicate what behaviors you would be most comfortable with on the continua below. Mark the appropriate place on the line for each item below.

1. Inviting people to be guests in your home:

◄──►

Anyone who seems to be a stranger in town.

Only friends you have known for a long time.

2. Your behavior toward a guest in your home:

◄──►

Behave however you feel – Regardless of how you make the guest feel.

Be accepting of the guest and make him or her comfortable – regardless of how you are feeling yourself.

3. Financial measures of hospitality:

◄──►

Serve a modest meal; the guest does not need to be entertained with fancy food and drink, even if your family is accustomed to dining elegantly

Serve the finest meal, even if you cannot afford such luxuries for your own family.

4. Limits of responsibility for guests:

◄──►

When the guest leaves your house, he is on his own.

You must escort your guest to his next destination to ensure his safety.

5. How to behave as a guest:

◄──►

Praise the hospitality regardless of its quality.

Praise the hospitality only if it conforms to your personal standards

PART TWO: ANALYZING HACHNASAT ORCHIM IN YOUR LIFE

Look at your answers on the Values Continua. How can you make (or continue to make) Hachnasat Orchim important in your life?

Read and discuss the following texts. Then answer the questions according to what the texts say.

וְכִי־יָגוּר אִתְּךָ גֵּר בְּאַרְצְכֶם לא תונו אתו׃ כְּאֶזְרָח מִכֶּם יִהְיֶה לָכֶם הַגֵּר | הַגָּר
אִתְּכֶם וְאָהַבְתָּ לוֹ כָּמוֹךָ כִּי־גֵרִים הֱיִיתֶם בְּאֶרֶץ מִצְרָיִם אֲנִי יְהוָה אֱלֹהֵיכֶם׃

When a stranger resides with you, you shall not wrong him. The stranger who resides with you shall be to you as one of your citizens; you shall love him as yourself, for you were strangers in the land of Egypt: I am the Lord am your God. V'ayikra 19:33-34

יהי ביתך פתוח לרוחה כיצד מלמד שיהא
ביתו של אדם פתוח לרוחה לדרום ולמזרח ולמערב ולצפון כגון (שעשה) איוב
שעשה ארבעה פתחים לביתו. ולמה עשה איוב ארבעה פתחים לביתו. כדי שלא
יהיו עניים מצטערים להקיף את כל הבית. הבא מן הצפון יכנס כדרכו הבא מן
הדרום יכנס כדרכו וכן לכל רוח לכך עשה איוב ארבעה פתחים לביתו.

Let your house be opened wide. How? This teaches that a man's house should have a wide entrance on the north, south, east, and west, like Job's, who made four doors to his house. And why did Job make four doors to his house? So that the poor would not be troubled to go all around the house: someone coming from the north could enter in his path, someone coming from the south could enter in his path, and so from all directions. For that reason Job made four doors to his house.
Avot d'Rabbi Natan 7A

כי הוה כרך ריפתא הוה פתח לבביה ואמר: כל מאן דצריך - ליתי וליכול.

When he [Rav Huna] would eat a meal, he would open his door wide and declare: "Whoever is in need, let him come and eat." Ta'anit 20b

עוד מנהג גדול היה בירושלים, מפה פרוסה על גבי הפתח כל
זמן שמפה פרוסה - אורחין נכנסין, נסתלקה המפה - אין האורחין נכנסין.

There was a fine custom in Jerusalem. At the commencement of a meal, a cloth was spread over the door of the house. So long as the cloth was spread, guests entered. When the cloth was removed, no guests entered. Baba Batra 93b

למוד בני ביתך ענוה שבזמן שאדם ענוותן ובני ביתו ענוותנין כשבא עני
ועמד על פתחו של בעל הבית ואמר להם אביכם יש בכאן יאמרו לו הן בא
והכנס עד שלא נכנס ושלחן [היה ערוך] לפניו נכנס ואכל ושתה וברך לשם
שמים נעשית לו נחת רוח גדולה. ובזמן שאדם ענוותן ובני ביתו קפדנין ובא
עני ועמד על פתחו ואמר להם אביכם יש בכאן ואומרים לו לא וגוערים בו
והוציאו בנזיפה.

Teach the members of your household humility. For when one is humble and his family members are humble, if a poor man comes and stands in the doorway of the master of the house and asks them, "Is your father inside?" they answer, "Yes, come in; enter." Even before he has entered, a table is set for him. When he enters and eats and offers a blessing up to heaven, the master of the house has great joy. But when one is not humble and the members of the household are short-tempered, if a poor man comes and stands in the doorway and inquires of them, "Is your father inside?" they answer, "No!" and rebuke him, driving him off in anger. Avot d'Rabbi Natan A7

These questions serve as guidelines for talking about how Hachnasat Orchim affects us in a modern day setting. Answer the following questions in column one based on your understanding of hospitality today and the second column according to the rabbinic texts you just read.

	HOSPITALITY TODAY	RABBINIC TEXTS
How might you make people feel welcome in your home?		
Should strangers and guests respond in any special way when you extend gestures of friendship and hospitality?		
How do you expect your guests to behave in order to show appreciation for your thoughtfulness?		
When you are a guest, are there aspects of a host's behavior that can make you feel uncomfortable?		

A FURTHER LOOK

As the Talmud illustrates, there is a great need for Hachnasat Orchim both within our own community and between different communities. Hachnasat Orchim involves two groups of people who each have a distinct role, the host and the guest. Jewish texts explicitly provide a values-based framework for the host and the guest. One way to fulfill the mitzvah of Hachnasat Orchim is to understand the expectations of the host and the guest.

Activity: The Good Host and the Good Guest

Read through the following texts. Then make a list of attributes of a good host and of a good guest. Try to think of times when you have exhibited those attributes as a host or as a guest, and times when you have not.

The Host

והוי שמח על שולחנך בשעה שהרעבין נהנין ממנה...

Be happy as you sit at your table and the hungry are enjoying your hospitality... Derech Eretz Zuta 9

ואין מסתכלין בפני האוכל ולא למנתו שלא לבישו.

The host was forbidden to embarrass his guest by watching them too attentively.
Mishneh Torah, Laws of Blessings, 7:6

מעשה ברבי אליעזר ורבי יהושע ורבי צדוק שהיו מסובין בבית המשתה בנו של רבן גמליאל, והיה רבן גמליאל עומד ומשקה עליהם.

Rabban Gamliel, the Nasi [the head of the Sanhedrin], served the guests at his son's wedding. (From this, we learn that hosts should honor guests by personally serving them.) Kiddushin 32b

Customarily, a person receives a guest. On the first day, the host serves him fowl; on the second day the host serves him meat; on the third day fish; on the next day cheese; on the next beans – diminishing until he serves greens. Pesikta d'Rav Kahana, ed. Buber, page 195b; Midrash Tehillim 23:3

כופין ללויה כדרך שכופין לצדקה, ובית דין היו מתקנין שלוחין ללוות אדם העובר ממקום למקום, ואם נתעצלו בדבר זה מעלה עליהם כאילו שפכו דמים

A person is required by the bet din [court] to escort guests...The bet din used to appoint guides to escort those who traveled from place to place. If the court was lax about this, its members were considered to be spillers of blood. Mishneh Torah, Laws of the Mourner, 14:3

	ATTRIBUTES OF A GOOD HOST	PERSONAL REAL LIFE EXAMPLES
1.		
2.		
3.		
4.		
5.		

The Guest

הוא היה אומר:
אורח טוב מהו אומר - כמה טרחות טרח בעל הבית בשבילי, כמה בשר הביא לפני, כמה יין הביא לפני, כמה גלוסקאות הביא לפני, וכל מה שטרח - לא טרח אלא בשבילי. אבל אורח רע מהו אומר - מה טורח טרח בעל הבית זה? פת אחת אכלתי, חתיכה אחת אכלתי, כוס אחד שתיתי, כל טורח שטרח בעל הבית זה - לא טרח אלא בשביל אשתו ובניו.

He [Ben Zoma], used to say, "What does a good guest say? 'How much trouble my host goes through for me! How much meat he has offered! How much wine he has set before me! How many cakes he has brought before me! And all this trouble he went thought only for me."

"But an inconsiderate guest, what does he say? 'What trouble has my host gone through? I've eaten one piece of bread and a single piece of meat. I've had but one cup of wine. All the trouble the host has gone to has been only for his family.'" Berachot 58a

הנכנס לבית כל מה שיגזר עליו בעל הבית יעשה.

The guest should comply with every request the host makes of him. Derech Eretz Rabbah 6

אמר רבי יהושע בן חנניה:
מימי לא נצחני אדם חוץ מאשה תינוק ותינוקת. אשה מאי היא? פעם אחת נתארחתי אצל אכסניא אחת, עשתה לי פולין. ביום ראשון אכלתים ולא שיירתי מהן כלום, שנייה ולא שיירתי מהן כלום. ביום שלישי הקדיחתן במלח. כיון שטעמתי - משכתי ידי מהן. אמרה לי: רבי, מפני מה אינך סועד? אמרתי לה: כבר סעדתי מבעוד יום. אמרה לי: היה לך למשוך ידיך מן הפת - אמרה לי: רבי, שמא לא הנחת פאה בראשונים? ולא כך אמרו חכמים: אין משיירין פאה באילפס, אבל משיירין פאה בקערה.

R. Joshua b. Hananiah remarked… "I was once staying at an inn where the hostess served me beans. On the first day, I ate all of them, leaving nothing. One the second day, too, I left nothing. On the third day, she over-seasoned them with salt, and as soon as I tasted them, I withdrew my hand. 'My master,' she said to me, 'why do you not eat?' 'I have eaten already,' I replied, 'earlier in the day.' 'You should, then,' she said to me, 'have withdrawn your hand from the bread. My master,' she continued, 'is it possible that you left the dish today as compensation for the former meals, for have not the Sages laid down the rule: Nothing is to be left in the pot, but something must be left on the plate?'"
Eruvin 53b

Guests should acknowledge the hospitality of their hosts by including a special section of the "Grace After Meals" in their honor. (Note that hospitality extended by parents is also acknowledged.)

הָרַחֲמָן הוּא יְבָרֵךְ אֶת-(אָבִי מוֹרִי) בַּעַל הַבַּיִת הַזֶּה וְאֶת-(אִמִּי מוֹרָתִי) בַּעֲלַת הַבַּיִת הַזֶּה אוֹתָם וְאֶת-בֵּיתָם וְאֶת-זַרְעָם וְאֶת-כָּל-אֲשֶׁר לָהֶם...

May the Merciful One bless (my father – my teacher) the head of this household, and (my mother – my teacher) the mistress of this household, their children, and all that is theirs… Birkat HaMazon

	ATTRIBUTES OF A GOOD GUEST	PERSONAL REAL LIFE EXAMPLES
1.		
2.		
3.		
4.		
5.		

PRACTICE MAKES PERFECT—IMPLEMENTING HACHNASAT ORCHIM IN OUR HOMES

The Invitation

- Who might be potential guests in your home?
- How should an invitation be extended?
- How should a guest respond to an invitation?

The Visit

- How should guests be entertained?
- What should the guest do and what should the host do during the course of the visit?
- How should the host act?

Saying Goodbye

- How should the visit be ended?
- How should the guest leave the home of a host?
- What should the guest and the host say to each other?

HACHNASAT ORCHIM IN OUR EVERYDAY LIVES

How many times have you been the "new kid on the block?" This is a very common situation for people. Remember going to a USY meeting, convention or summer program when you didn't know anyone? Everyone has been or will be that person at one time in their life. Often we forget what it was like to be that person. When doing the next exercise try to think back to a time when you were either the "new kid on the block," or when you were the person who encountered the "new kid on the block."

Ally and Mike are members of USY. They regularly attend services on Shabbat and know the other congregants and USY members fairly well. One Friday night they noticed an unfamiliar face among the group attending services. A teenager that they had never seen before was sitting alone near the rear of the synagogue. A number of their friends were gathered near the front of the synagogue, waiting for the services to begin. Ally and Mike exchanged puzzled glances about the presence of the stranger; they were not comfortable about ignoring him.

- ➤ **What might Ally and Mike be thinking?**
- ➤ **What might the teenager sitting in the back of the synagogue be thinking?**
- ➤ **What would be an appropriate way for Ally and Mike to react to this situation?**
- ➤ **Write an ending to this anecdote: what should Ally and Mike do?**

HACHNASAT ORCHIM: A GLOBAL PERSPECTIVE

We have looked at Hachnasat Orchim from a personal perspective, but there is also a global perspective to Hachnasat Orchim. As discussed earlier, the value of Hachnasat Orchim is not only emphasized by Judaism for within our own familial and Jewish communities, but also for our relationship building with other communities around the world.

> "The tradition of hospitality was particularly apparent among Jewish communities in the Middle Ages and a separate charitable association called *Hevra Hachnasat Orchim* was established for that purpose. Medieval European Jewish communities instituted the idea of a *pletten* ("meal tickets") for travelers and itinerant scholars, and in the 15th century, established *battei bahurim* ("student hostels"). Nor was individual hospitality neglected; Nathan Hannover (17th century) states: 'Many wealthy members of the congregation considered it an honor to have the student and his charges as guests at their table, although the congregation sufficiently provided for their support' (Yeven Mezulah…). Among Polish communities, it was also the custom to billet students with members of the community for their daily meals…This custom, known as *essenteg,* later spread to Germany." "Hospitality." Encyclopedia Judaica, 1972. VIII, 1032-33

RABBI YANNAI'S QUIZ

> *Once Rabbi Yannai was walking along a road and he saw a well-dressed man. Thinking the man to be a great man and a scholar, Rabbi Yannai said to him, "Would the rabbi honor me and be a guest in my house?" The man replied, "Yes."*
>
> *Rabbi Yannai took the man into his home and gave him food and drink. He then quizzed the guest in Mishnah, Aggadah, and Talmud. The man was ignorant of all. Rabbi Yannai then said, "Wash your hands and say Birkat HaMazon [Grace After Meals]." The man replied, "Let Yannai say Birkat HaMazon in his own house" (because he did not know how to recite the prayer). Rabbi Yannai said, "Repeat after me: 'A dog has eaten from Yannai's bread.'" The guest jumped up, grabbed Yannai and said, "My inheritance is with you and you would keep it from me!" "How," asked the rabbi, "is your inheritance with me?" The guest replied, "Once, when passing a schoolhouse, I heard the children saying:* Torah tzivah lanu Moshe, morasha kehillat Ya'akov.*' [Moses commanded the Torah to us, it is the inheritance of the community of Jacob (Devarim 33:4).]* 'Morashah kehillat Yannai' *[it is the inheritance of the community of Yannai] it does* not *say, but rather* 'kehillat Ya'akov' *[Jacob's community]!"*

When the two men were reconciled, Rabbi Yannai asked, "How, then, are you worthy to eat at my table?" and the guest replied, "Never have I heard an evil word spoken against me and returned to argue with the person who spoke it. Never have I seen two people arguing without making peace between them." Rabbi Yannai then said, "You have so much derech eretz [proper behavior and respect] and I called you a dog!..."
Vayikra Rabbah Tzav 9

Can You Solve Yannai's Quiz?

1. What kind of person did Yannai want to invite to his home?
2. How was Yannai accustomed to treating his guests?
3. Is Yannai's request, "Wash your hands and say Birkat HaMazon" part of the quiz?
4. How did the guest do on Yannai's "quiz"?
5. Why do you think Yannai asked the guest to repeat the words, "A dog has eaten from Yannai's bread"?
6. How did the guest respond to the insult?
7. What did the guest do that impressed Yannai?

Yannai's Answers

1. Yannai wanted to invite a great man; a scholar to his house.
2. Yannai fed his guests and then quizzed them on their Jewish knowledge.
3. Yannai included his request to wash his hands and say Birkat HaMazon to find out if his guest knew how to behave properly at a meal and if he knew how to recite Birkat HaMazon.
4. Rabbi Yannai felt that his guest failed his quiz completely.
5. Yannai asked the guest to repeat the words about the dog because he was angry that his guest not only was not a scholar but also seemed to be completely ignorant of Jewish observance. Yannai must have considered the guest unworthy of his hospitality, since asking the guest to say that he was a dog was obviously an insult. Apparently, Yannai wanted his guest to know that he (the guest) did not live up to his (Yannai's) expectations.
6. Yannai's guest responded to the insult by explaining to Yannai that both of them have an equal share in the inheritance of the Jewish people. Yannai's learning did not entitle him to demean others simply because they did not possess his knowledge. The Torah was given to all the people of Israel—not only the people of Yannai!
7. The guest impressed Yannai by explaining his selfless concern for other people's sensitivities and for maintaining peace between people wherever he went.

A LESSON LEARNED

Yannai learned many lessons from his guest that evening. Among those were:

- Not to judge people by external appearances
- To offer hospitality without "strings" attached
- People should treat each other with derech eretz (respect, manners, sensitivity)
- To behave with derech eretz toward his guests

HEVRE HACHNASAT ORCHIM

Many synagogues have a more modern day version of the Hevre Hachnasat Orchim who work with new families. Over the last several years, synagogues have grappled with the question of whether or not to open their doors to refugees from other countries who have escaped the death and persecution on their doorstep, only to arrive in the United States to find that they have nowhere to go.

Convene a meeting of your synagogue Hevre Hachnasat Orchim. Should you allow these refugees to find shelter in your community with the support of the synagogue? Why or why not should your synagogue/community be responsible for these refugees? What about new people who come to the synagogue for the first time? Refer back to the Jewish texts that you learned earlier. Use those texts to help in making your decision.

The Jewish community is involved in organized Hachnasat Orchim. A modern day adaptation of the Hevra Hachnasat Orchim is HIAS (Hebrew Immigrant Aid Society).

HIAS INC. (Hebrew Immigrant Aid Society)

HIAS is a worldwide migration agency that rescues Jews from oppression in various countries and resettles them in places where they can live in dignity. HIAS dates back to 1884. It merged with the United Service for New Americans and the Migration Services of American Joint Distribution Committee to form the world-wide Jewish migration agency with offices, affiliates and committees in more than 40 countries including the United States, Europe, North Africa, Latin America, Canada, Australia, and New Zealand.

Program of Assistance: Provides a broad program of service for refugees and migrants. At the pre-migration stage this covers immigration counseling, visa documentation, representation and intervention before governmental and intergovernmental agencies, transportation, reception and related services. In addition, HIAS' worldwide location service assists in locating relatives and friends – sometimes separated for more than 50 years.

In the country of resettlement, HIAS, together with national and local agencies, facilitates reception of the migrants, reunion with families, initial adjustment, and adjustment of status and naturalization. Resettlement services provided by cooperation agencies in local communities also include professional counseling, care and maintenance's, language and citizenship training. Many also facilitate attendance at summer camps, day care nurseries for children of working mothers, the Jewish education of children of migrants, vocational guidance, sheltered workshops, and interest-free loans. Frequently these services are enhanced by community volunteers.

The United Synagogue Youth supports HIAS through the Tikun Olam funds. These funds provide a scholarship for a new Jewish immigrant to pursue college or vocational studies.

- **Can you cite any other examples of organizations showing Hachnasat Orchim?**

A Greater Understanding of Love Your Neighbor as Yourself

Treat your guests as you would want to be treated when you are a guest.

> FYI
> The word Bikur comes from the Hebrew root B-K-R, meaning to visit. The word Holim literally means sick [people].

WHAT IS BIKUR HOLIM?

Chances are, that you have performed an act of Bikur Holim before in your life. Think of a time when you went to visit a friend at home who was sick in bed, or a grandparent who fell ill and had to be hospitalized, or even just spent time at a hospital visiting with people that you never knew before! Bikur Holim is not always an easy way to become emotionally involved in your community, but the rewards are endless!

In modern times, the mitzvah of Bikur Holim has largely become a mitzvah for professionals. When a person becomes ill, he is treated by a network of health care facilities and medical professionals. In addition, he is generally visited by a clergyman of his faith or a social worker, who brings comfort to patients in local hospitals and nursing facilities. The question we need to ask ourselves is why? Why don't more people become involved in Bikur Holim? Do you have to be clergy or a social worker to practice Bikur Holim? Can anyone become involved in Bikur Holim?

EXERCISE: Who Needs Bikur Holim?

Sometimes it is hard to see a loved one; a friend or a family member sick in a hospital, or even at home. Visits can often be awkward, in that it is hard to judge what to say, and how to say it.

If you have ever been sick, what were your needs when people came to visit you?

____

____

____

____

List 10 needs of a sick person. Think of 10 topics or questions to discuss with loved ones when you see them in a hospital. These should be based on what you think a sick person wants or needs.

	Needs of someone who is sick	Topics/Questions to discuss during your visit
1.		
2.		
3.		
4.		
5.		
6.		
7.		
8.		
9.		
10.		

JUDAISM TEACHES US ABOUT BIKUR HOLIM

For centuries, Jews sought to give emotional support to those who were ill as well as to provide medical care to the extent that it was available. Jewish tradition deems that a community is responsible for it's own—including the old, the weak, and the frail. Bikur Holim is a manifestation of that principle of Judaism.

In Biblical Times...

One of our first introductions to Bikur Holim in the Torah is found in Bereshit 18 when after being circumcised at the age of 99, God sends 3 angels to visit Abraham at his tent.

> *God appeared to him [Abraham] in the plains of Mamre while he was sitting at the entrance of the tent in the heat of the day. He lifted his eyes and saw: And behold! three men were standing over him.* Bereshit 18:1-2

The Rabbis connect this chapter with the preceding, and declare that God visited Abraham while he recovered from his circumcision. From this passage, they deduce the duty of visiting the sick.

In the Middle Ages...

Much tenderness was shown in visiting those who were confined to their houses by prostrating illness. After synagogue service on the Sabbath morning, the worshippers paid regular visits to the sick before returning home to partake of their meal. This general concern with such matters partly accounts for the fact that so little parish visiting was done by the Rabbis in the middle ages; this function was performed by the laity in general and by lay-heads of the congregation in particular. The Rabbi merely performed his share like other pious members of the community.

The Jewish etiquette at such visits was almost beyond praise. It was thought bad manners for any but his most familiar friends to call upon the patient too soon after he fell ill, for such precipitancy might make him appear in a worse plight than he actually was. No visitor was to become a nuisance by making too long a stay; nor was he to present himself when the sufferer was in acute pain. The patient was to be cheered, and not depressed by conversation on dismal topics of death and misfortune. A mans' personal enemy was to refrain from visiting the sufferer, for his presence might be misconstrued as implying a desire to gloat over his foe's prostration. An essential of the visit was the prayer uttered on the patient's behalf.

It does not seem that the community found it necessary to make its own arrangements for the medical treatment of the poor until a late period. The Jewish physicians attended the poor without charge, a physician would train his son to regard that as the proper course of conduct, and at all times Jewish doctors charged very moderately for their services...Saul Astruc Cohen, a popular physician and scholar of Algiers at the close of the fourteenth century, not only practiced his art gratuitously, 'but spent his fortune in relieving both Mohammedan and Jewish poor.' A medical officer was often attached to a benevolent society...Such societies were chiefly called into existence by the various epidemics which devastated Europe in the Middle Ages. Under the strain of extraordinary needs, the usual methods for providing medical attendance broke down, and benevolent societies sprang into existence as rapidly as the demand for them arose. **Israel Abrahams, *Jewish Life in the Middle Ages*, Philadelphia: The Jewish Publication Society of America, 1958, pp. 329-331**

And Today...

Project Ezra on New York's Lower East Side provides for the many elderly Jews who continue to live in this once-bustling center of Jewish life. For many of the people Project Ezra serves, the staff of dedicated workers and volunteers are all that they have. They may be the sole survivors in a family or, perhaps, their family has scattered to other parts of the country. Project Ezra's efforts are vast. The only hot food many will eat is the daily meal that is either delivered to their homes or served at the local center. The food pantry at the local synagogue is also vital to the community. At Passover, it provides the standard fare, be it matzah, gefilte fish, or other items. Most donations provide for home health care—a critical ingredient that allows many elderly people to remain living independently at home rather than being forced into a nursing facility.

USY SUMMER PROGRAMS

Each summer, teenagers on USY Israel Pilgrimage and USY on Wheels visit hospitals on Friday afternoon before Shabbat to bring hallah, flowers and smiles to the patients before Shabbat begins.

CUDDLERS GIVE EXTRA CARE

> A premature baby lies waiting in a plastic cradle, much like all the other babies in the large, quiet hospital rooms. Balloons and stuffed animals decorate the silent space where only the beeping of monitors and an occasional whisper can be heard. In walks one of 225 volunteers who gently lifts the five-pound baby boy and sits back to rock him in a nearby chair. This is the first visit the baby has had in three days.
>
> Cuddlers work with infants, toddlers and children up to 18 years old staying in the hospital and perform many tasks. They hold, rock and sometimes feed the infants. They can also caress the babies, change the babies' diapers and sing and hum softly to them. Most nurses don't have the time to be one on one with the children and some of the parents live out of town so they can't drive to see the babies every day. Research has proven that human contact is necessary for nurturing and developing a trusting relationship, and the Cuddlers provide that contact when the parents are absent. Providing constant attention to these babies who remain in the hospital for long stays is not always possible, and that is where the Cuddlers come in.
>
> **Adapted from "Cuddlers Give Extra Care to Shands' Kids by Christine Martinez de Castro**

- ➢ What are some of the common values that are espoused in all three time periods?
- ➢ Do you think there are certain groups of people who are more responsible than others to perform Bikur Holim?
- ➢ Do you feel a responsibility to do Bikur Holim?

WHY DO WE VISIT THE SICK?

- ➢ What is so important about visiting the sick?
- ➢ Why do you think that it is such an important mitzvah?
- ➢ How can Bikur Holim strengthen the community that you live in?

How does knowing that the Jewish community cherishes the value of helping those in need make you feel—as a potential recipient of the help? as a donor, representing the community? Does the Jewish value of helping those in need represent a position on the dependence/interdependence issue? Use ideas you have studied from Jewish tradition to prove what you believe about the values of the Jewish community.

READING THE TEXT CRITICALLY

FYI: A FEW DEFINITIONS

The following several sections use Jewish texts to answer important questions about Bikur Holim. Note: There are some original texts in this chapter. There is a page of the Shulhan Aruch supplemented by the individual translations. The Shulhan Aruch is a law code written by Joseph Karo. Its name means "a set table" and it was written to help the masses of the Jewish people understand what was considered by the authorities of the mid-16th century to be proper practice according to halacha: Jewish law. It is a digest of Jewish law, generally presenting the conclusions of halachic discussions but not the arguments that led to the conclusions. Karo was a Sephardic Jew (i.e., from the Meditteranean basin). After he wrote his code, a rabbi by the name of Moses Isserles wrote comments on each section where the customs of the Ashkenazic community (i.e., Jews living in Eastern Europe) differed from those of the Sephardim. As a result, the Shulhan Aruch together with the notes by Isserles reflected Jewish law as it was practiced in all of the then-known Jewish world. [Adapted from Eliot Dorff, *Conservative Judaism: Our Ancestors to Our Descendents,* New York: United Synagogue Youth, 1996]

There is also a page of Talmud in this chapter. The Talmud is the central pillar supporting the entire spiritual and intellectual way of Jewish life. The Talmud, in the broader sense of the term, is made up of two components: the Mishnah, which is the first written summary of the Oral Law, and the Gemara (called Talmud in the more restricted sense of the term), which is formally an explanation and commentary on the Mishnah.

The Talmud was created from generation to generation. Certain questions, either collective or raised by an individual scholar and cited in his name, together with the answers to them, became part of the treasure-house of knowledge of every scholar. He had to remember the questions raised regarding particular Mishnayot and their answers. These questions and answers and their study in one generation were passed on to the next. Later other problems would arise and be transmitted to the following generation as the remembered tradition of the previous one. At the end of the 4th century, CE, the process began to record the Talmud, and took more than 150 years to complete. [Adapted from Adin Steinsaltz, *The Talmud: The Steinsaltz Edition, A Reference Guide,* New York: Random House, 1989]

Read the first line of the following text from Nedarim 39b:

אמר רבי אחא בר חנינא: כל המבקר חולה - נוטל אחד מששים בצערו.

Rabbi Aha son of Hanina said: "He who visits an invalid takes away a sixtieth of his pain."

- How would you react to the idea that each person who visits someone that is not well takes away 1/60th of their illness. Is it true?
- What could the Rabbis have had in mind?
- If someone believed this idea, then what would he do every time someone got sick?

Now continue reading the text:

אמרי ליה: אם כן, ליעלון שיתין ולוקמוה

They said to him: "If so, let sixty people visit him and restore him to health!"

➢ **Do you think the Rabbis considered a person's illness actually to decrease because many people came to visit them?**

Resume reading the text to see how Rabbi Aha bar Hanina explained himself:

אמר ליה: כעישורייתא דבי רבי, ובבן גילו דתניא, רבי אומר: בת הניזונית מנכסי אחין נוטלת עישור נכסים, אמרו לו לרבי: לדבריך, מי שיש לו עשר בנות ובן, אין לו לבן במקום בנות כלום אמר להן: ראשונה נוטלת עישור נכסים, שניה - במה ששיירה, שלישית - במה ששיירה, וחוזרות וחולקות בשוה.

He replied: "The [principal of decreasing illness by a] sixtieth is [the same principal of distribution of property among female heirs:] as the tenth spoken of in the school of Rabbi...For it was taught: Rabbi said, "A daughter who enjoys maintenance from her brother's estate receives a tenth of that estate." Said they to Rabbi: "If so, if a man leaves ten daughters and one son, the latter receives nothing!" He replied: "The first (to marry) receives a tenth of the estate; the second a tenth of the remaining; the third, a tenth of what remains."

The people first indicate that since every visitor decreases the remaining part of the illness by 1/60th, then if the room was filled with 60 people, the person's health could be restored. However, Rabbi Aha son of Hanina continued to explain that while the first person can take away 1/60th of his pain, the ones to follow would only take away a percentage of what is left.

➢ **What do you think they were trying to teach in this text? Think about the feelings of the sick person, how visitors can take the sick person's mind of their pain, and how visitors can provide a link to the outside world.**

The next portion of the text relates a story about how the sage Rabbi Akiba taught his disciples about the mitzvah of Bikur Holim.

> רב חלבו חלש, נפק אכריז רב כהנא:
> רב חלבו באיש, לא איכא דקא אתי. אמר להו: לא כך היה מעשה? בתלמיד אחד מתלמידי ר' עקיבא שחלה, לא נכנסו חכמים לבקרו, ונכנס ר' עקיבא לבקרו, ובשביל שכיבדו וריבצו לפניו חיה, א"ל: רבי, החייתני! יצא ר' עקיבא ודרש: כל מי שאין מבקר חולים - כאילו שופך דמים.
>
> *Rav Helbo fell ill. Thereupon Rav Kahana went and proclaimed: "Rav Helbo is sick." But no one visited him. He rebuked them (the scholars), saying, "Did it not once happen that one of Rabbi Akiba's disciples fell sick, and the Sages did not visit him? So Rabbi Akiba himself entered (his house) to visit him, and because they swept and sprinkled the ground before him, he recovered. 'My master,' he said, 'you have revived me!' Rabbi Akiba went forth and lectured: 'He who does not visit the sick is like a shedder of blood.'"*

➢ **What was it that Rabbi Akiba did for his disciple?**

➢ **How could this action have caused the man to recover?**

➢ **Do you agree with Akiba's conclusion: "He who does not visit the sick is like a shedder of blood?"**

Following is the conclusion of this selection from the Talmud:

> כי אתא רב דימי אמר: כל המבקר את החולה - גורם לו שיחיה, וכל שאינו מבקר את החולה - גורם לו שימות. מאי גרמא? אילימא כל המבקר את החולה - מבקש עליו רחמים שיחיה, וכל שאין מבקר את החולה - מבקש עליו רחמים שימות, שימות ס"ד? אלא, כל שאין מבקר חולה - אין מבקש עליו רחמים לא שיחיה ולא שימות.
>
> *When Rav Dimi came, he said: "He who visits the sick causes him to live, while he who does not causes him to die." How does he cause (this)? Shall we say that he who visits the sick prays that he may live, while he who does not prays that he should die? – "That he should die!" Can you really think (someone would pray) so? But (say thus): "He who does not visit the sick prays neither that he may live nor die."*

➢ **After reading the different parts of this text from the Talmud, why, according to the rabbis, should we visit the sick?**

FOR HOW LONG SHOULD I VISIT?

אמר רב שישא בריה דרב אידי: לא ליסעוד איניש קצירא לא בתלת שעי קדמייתא ולא בתלת שעי בתרייתא דיומא, כי היכי דלא ליסח דעתיה מן רחמי. תלת שעי קדמייתא - רווחא דעתיה, בתרייתא - תקיף חולשיה.

Rav Shisha son of Rav Idi said: "One should not visit the sick during the first three or the last three hours (of the day), lest he thereby omit to pray for him." During the first three house of the day his (the invalid's) illness is alleviated; in the last three hours, his sickness is strongest. Nedarim 40a

➢ What are the two reasons given for not visiting the sick during the first and last three hours of the day?

➢ Why shouldn't a visitor see the sick person when they are feeling at their best or at their worst?

Think about this: If a person sees someone who is sick during the first three hours, they might think that the sick person is nearly well and not in need of visitors. If he visits during the last three hours, they might think that the patient is about to die. In either case, the temporary change in the sick person's condition might cause the visitor to treat him in ways that are inappropriate to his condition.

➢ Why do you think that the Rabbis felt that they needed to say this explicitly? Doesn't it seem obvious?

WHO AM I RESPONSIBLE TO VISIT?

Judah HeHasid, a 12th century moralist, declared:

עני חולה ועשיר חולה ורבים הולכים לעשיר לכבדו
תלך אתה אצל העני אפי' אם עשיר תלמיד חכם.

If a poor man and a rich man fall ill at the same time, and many go to the rich man to pay him honor, then go to the poor man, even if the rich man is a scholar."
Reuben Margoliot, ed., *Sefer Hasidim* (1956), p. 267, no. 361

➢ Why, according to the text, should people go to visit sick people who they may not even know?

➢ Isn't it enough to just visit the sick that are our friends and relatives?

Read the following text from the Jerusalem Talmud:

הקרובים נכנסים אצלו מיד והרחוקים נכנסים אצלו לאחר ג' ימים

Relatives (and close friends) visit as soon as a person becomes ill. Others should visit after the first three days of illness. Jerusalem Talmud Pe'ah 18a

It seems that there is a preference for visitors who are closely acquainted with the sick person during the early days of the illness. Can you think of some reasons for this preference? Do you think there is any connection between this thought and the notion that visitors should not see the invalid during certain hours of the day?

WHOM NOT TO VISIT

אמר שמואל: אין מבקרין את החולה אלא למי
שחלצתו חמה. לאפוקי מאי? לאפוקי הא דתניא, ר' יוסי בן פרטא אומר משום
ר' אליעזר: אין מבקרין לא חולי מעיים ולא חולי העין ולא מחושי הראש.
בשלמא חולי מעיים משום כיסופא, אלא חולי העין ומחושי הראש מ"ט? משום
דרב יהודה, דאמר רב יהודה: דיבורא קשיא לעינא ומעלי לאישתא.

Samuel said: "Only a sick person who is feverish may be visited." What does this exclude? It excludes those concerning whom it has been taught by R. Yose ben Parta in R. Eliezer's name: "One must not visit those suffering with bowel trouble, or with eye disease or from headaches." Now, the first is logical, the reason being through embarrassment; but what is the reason of the other two? On account of Rav Judah's dictum: "Speech is injurious to the eyes and to people suffering from headaches."
Nedarim 41a

- What modern diseases might fit in this category?
- Does this mean not to visit such a person at all?
- How is this passage influenced by what the Rabbis said about decreasing illness by visiting?

WHAT DO I DO WHEN I'M VISITING SOMEONE WHO IS SICK?

Note: If you are using this book with a group of people, consider studying the following texts in *hevruta* (partners). Then, have one person in the *hevruta* act as the visitor according to the texts, and have the other person act as the sick person, according to the texts.

If you are studying this on your own, try to imagine the patient/visitor relationship as outlined in these texts.

- Do the suggestions provided by the Jewish texts help your visit?
- Or do they make the role of the visitor more difficult when visiting?

רבי יהודה אומר: המקום ירחם עליך ועל חולי ישראל. רבי יוסי אומר:
המקום ירחם עליך בתוך חולי ישראל.
דרבי אלעזר... זימנין אמר המקום יפקדך
לשלום וזימנין אמר (ליה) רחמנא ידכרינך לשלם.

When Rabbi Judah visited the sick, he said, "May the Almighty have compassion upon you and upon the sick of Israel." Rabbi Yose said, "May the Almighty have compassion upon you in the midst of the sick of Israel." ...Sometimes Rabbi Elazar would say, "The Almighty visit you in peace." At other times he said, "The Almighty remembers you in peace." **Shabbat 12b**

Note the attitude of the Rabbis toward helping each other when they were ill:

רבי חייא בר אבא חלש,
על לגביה רבי יוחנן. אמר ליה: חביבין עליך יסורין? אמר ליה: לא הן ולא שכרן.
אמר ליה: הב לי ידך. יהב ליה ידיה ואוקמיה. רבי יוחנן חלש, על לגביה רבי
חנינא. אמר ליה: חביבין עליך יסורין? אמר ליה: לא הן ולא שכרן. אמר ליה: הב
לי ידך. יהב ליה ידיה ואוקמיה. אמאי? לוקים רבי יוחנן לנפשיה - אמרי: אין
חבוש מתיר עצמו מבית האסורים.

Rabbi Hiyya b. Abba fell ill and Rabbi Yohanan went in to visit him. He said to him: "Are your sufferings welcome to you?" He replied: "Neither they nor their reward." He said to him: "Give me your hand." He gave him his hand and he raised him.

R. Yohanan once fell ill and Rabbi Hanina went in to visit him. He said to him: "Are your sufferings welcome to you?" He replied: "Neither they nor their reward." He said to him: "Give me your hand." He gave him his and and he raised him. Why could not R. Yohanan raise himself? —They replied: "The prisoner cannot free himself from jail." Berachot 5b

When you visit a sick man who is without means, do not go to him with empty hands. When he awakes be quick to offer refreshments to him and he will esteem it as though you did uphold and restore his soul.
Rabbi Eliezer of Worms
Abrahams, *Hebrew Ethical Wills*, p.44,

LAWS OF VISITING THE SICK

שלחן ערוך יורה דעה סימן שלה

מתי מבקרין החולה ואיזה חולים מבקרין וכיצד מתפללין עליו?

א מצוה לבקר חולים הקרובים והחברים נכנסים מיד והרחוקים אחר ג׳ ימים ואם קפץ עליו החולי אלו ואלו נכנסים מיד. *(טור בקיצור מס׳ ת״ה להרמב״ן):*

ב אפי׳ הגדול ילך לבקר הקטן ואפילו כמה פעמים ביום ואפילו בן גילו וכל המוסיף ה״ז משובח *ובלבד שלא יטריח לו: הגה* י״א דשונא יכול לילך לבקר חולה (מהרי״ל קצ״ז) ולא נראה לי אלא לא *יבקר חולה ולא ינחם אבל שהוא שונאו שלא יחשב ששמח לאידו ואינו לו אלא צער. כן נראה לי (ש״ס פ׳ כ״ג):*

ג המבקר את החולה לא ישב ע״ג מטה ולא ע״ג כסא ולא ע״ג ספסל אלא מתעטף ויושב לפניו שהשכינה למעלה מראשותיו: *הגה ודוקא כשהחולה שוכב על הארץ דהיושב גבוה ממנו אבל כשוכב על המטה מותר לישב על כסא וספסל (ב״י בשם הר״ן והגהות מיימוני ותוס׳ והג״א) וכן נהגין:*

ד אין מבקרין החולה בג׳ שעות ראשונות של יום מפני שכל חולה מיקל עליו חליו בבקר ולא יחוש לבקש עליו רחמים ולא בג׳ שעות אחרונות של יום שאז מכביד עליו חליו ויתייאש מלבקש עליו רחמים *(וכל שביקר ולא ביקש עליו רחמים לא קיים המצוה) (ב״י בשם הרמב״ן):*

ה כשמבקש עליו רחמים אם מבקש לפניו יכול לבקש בכל לשון שירצה ואם מבקש שלא בפניו לא יבקש אלא בלשון הקדש:

ו יכלול אותו בתוך חולי ישראל שיאמר המקום ירחם עליך בתוך חולי ישראל ובשבת אומר שבת היא מלזעוק ורפואה קרובה לבא:

ז אומרים לו שיתן דעתו על ענייניו אם הלוה או הפקיד אצל אחרים או אחרים הלוו או הפקידו אצלו ואל יפחד מפני זה מהמות:

ח אין מבקרין לא לחולי מעים ולא לחולי העין ולא לחולי הראש וכן לכל חולי דתקיף ליה עלמא וקשה ליה דיבורא אין מבקרין אותו בפניו אלא נכנסין בבית החיצון ושואלים ודורשין בו אם צריכין לכבד ולדבץ לפניו וכיוצא בו ושומעין צערו ומבקשים עליו רחמים:

ט מבקרין חולי עובדי כוכבים מפני דרכי שלום:

י בחולי מעים אין האיש משמש את האשה אבל האשה משמשת את האיש: *הגה י״א שמי שיש לו חולה בביתו ילך אצל חכם שבעיר שיבקש עליו רחמים (ב״י פ׳ י״ג) וכן נהגו לברך חולים בב״ה לקרא להם שם חדש כי שינוי השם קורע גזר דינו ניחום אבלים קודם לבקור חולים (כל בו):*

Shulhan Aruch, Yoreh De'ah 335

When do we visit the sick? Which sick do we visit? How do we pray for them?

1. It is a mitzvah to visit the sick. Relatives and friends should visit as soon as the person becomes ill. More distant acquaintances should wait to visit until 3 days after the onset of the illness. If the sickness came upon him suddenly, relatives, friends, and more distant acquaintances should all visit immediately.

2. Even an important person should visit one who is less important, even many times during the day [even one born under the same sign]. Those who visit frequently are to be praised, as long as they do not burden the invalid. *(Isserles: Some people say that even an enemy should visit an invalid. But it seems to me that an enemy should neither visit the sick nor comfort the mourner lest it be thought that he is rejoicing over their misfortune.)*

3. He who visits the sick should not sit on the bed, on a chair, or on a bench. He should cover himself and sit before the invalid (at his feet) inasmuch as the Shechinah (God's presence) rests about his head. *(Isserles: ...especially when the invalid lies on the ground, so that the visitor should not be seated higher than he is. But if the invalid lies on a bed, the visitor may sit on a chair or a bench.)*

4. We do not visit the sick during the first 3 hours of the day, because in the early morning his sickness is not as harsh as it is normally, and we might think it unnecessary to ask for God's compassion for him. Neither do we visit during the last 3 hours of the day when the illness weighs upon him most heavily because we might despair and not ask for God's compassion [thinking the condition is hopeless]. *(Isserles: A visitor who does not ask for God's compassion for the invalid has not fulfilled the mitzvah or Bikur Holim.)*

5. When the visitor asks for God's compassion – if he prays in front of the invalid, he may pray in any language he desires. But if he prays no in the presence of the invalid, then he should pray only in the Hebrew language.

6. The visitor includes the invalid among the sick of Israel saying (in his prayer): May God have compassion upon you among the sick of Israel. On Shabbat the visitor's prayer is: Shabbat prevents one from crying out and healing will come soon.

7. The visitors tell the invalid to put his affairs in order if he has lent or deposited funds with others or if they have lent or deposited funds with him. Even so, the invalid should not fear that his death is imminent.

8. We do not visit those that are ill with sickness of the stomach, the eye, the head, or any serious illness, or if it is difficult for him to speak. We do not visit him in person but we enter an anteroom, inquire if he needs anything (such as help cleaning), listen to his trouble, and pray for him.

9. We visit the sick among non-Jews in order to keep peace.

10. Concerning intestinal ailments, a man does not attend to a woman, but a woman does attend to a man. *(Isserles: Some say that if there is an invalid in one's home, he should go to a scholar in his town and ask for compassion for the invalid. It was customary to bless the sick in the synagogue and to give them new names since changing one's names changes his harsh decree. Comforting mourners takes precedence over visiting the sick.)*

- After learning about all the different Jewish perspectives on Bikur Holim, do you think the vast resources and availability of medical care in the 21th century will affect the mitzvah of Bikur Holim? If so, how?

- Think back to the text when God visits Abraham in the book of Genesis. Are our principles behind Bikur Holim the same today, as they were in Biblical times? Why or why not?

OUR PERSONAL RELATIONSHIP WITH BIKUR HOLIM

Consideration of how modern Jewish communities can practice Bikur Holim is extremely important. Inasmuch as complete health care—including giving comfort and emotional support to the sick—is available through the service of professionals, what should be the role of lay people in Bikur Holim?

- Can volunteers succeed in helping the patients in ways that professionals (rabbis, chaplains) generally cannot succeed?
- Moreover, as a high school student, can I really help patients in ways that professionals (Rabbis, chaplains) generally cannot succeed?

Absolutely!

In fact, over the past few years there have been mitzvah heroes all over the world who are even younger than high school who have been involved in Bikur Holim on a large scale!

Bikur Holim is one of the most easily accessible mitzvot. It is a great way to get involved in your community and to take part in making someone's life a little bit nicer!

Exercise: Thinking about Bikur Holim

List some ways you can fulfill the Mitzvah of Bikur Holim

As Individuals	In a Group

A Greater Understanding of Love Your Neighbor as Yourself

Would you like visitors when you are ill or need help?

The prosperity of a country is in accordance with the treatment of the aged.

Rabbi Nachman of Braslov

FOCUS ON MYRIAM MENDILOW: MITZVAH HERO

Those who knew Jerusalem in the early days of the State will no doubt recall the elderly beggars who lined the streets, unwashed, ragged and despairing. It was a time when all energies and meager finances then available were directed entirely to security needs and the urgency of absorbing the thousands of new immigrants flocking to the country. Social welfare was still a concept of the future. Turmoil and an almost chaotic newness excluded these pressing concerns.

One woman decided that something must be done. Mrs. Myriam Mendilow, born in Safed, was a teacher at the French Alliance Israelite school in the poor neighborhood of Musrara. She was determined to dedicate herself to improving the lives of these destitute beggars in the neighborhood where she taught. Her first attempts to befriend them were not successful until she organized a holiday (Tu B'shevat) party with the help of the local rabbi. She brought in food and entertainment, and won their trust and appreciation. Soon after, she gave up her teaching career to devote her life to helping the poor and elderly, and to educate the young to respect and love them.

In 1962, Myriam Mendelow founded Lifeline for the Old (Yad Lakashish) in order to provide needy elderly and disabled Jerusalemites with the opportunity to spend their days productively and in good company. "To be is to do" was her motto and continues to be Lifeline's philosophy today. The first workshop established was the Bookbindery, to repair and rebind text books from the local schools creating the connecting link between the young and old. To this day, the Bookbindery exists and flourishes along with eight additional workshops. Presently, some 250 elderly and disabled individuals receive "on the job training" and supervision and produce high quality ceramics, weaving, embroidery, woodwork, and many other crafts. The participants receive a small stipend, and the income from the sale of their products supports a wide range of auxiliary services provided by the organization.

WHAT IS THE JEWISH TRADITION OF HIDDUR P'NAI ZAKEN?

אַל־תַּשְׁלִיכֵנִי לְעֵת זִקְנָה כִּכְלוֹת כֹּחִי אַל־תַּעַזְבֵנִי

Do not cast me off in old age; when my strength fails, do not forsake me! Tehillim 71:9

This prayer, recited especially on Yom Kippur, is addressed not to man, but to God; it is a plea that can also be answered through fulfillment by other Jews of their moral obligations to honor their parents and to care for those in need of help.

- Why do you think that this prayer is recited on Yom Kippur?
- What connection does it have with Yom Kippur?

והזהרו בזקן ששכח תלמודו מחמת אונסו. דאמרינן: לוחות ושברי לוחות מונחות בארון.

Even the old man who has forgotten his learning must be treated tenderly, for were not the broken tablets placed in the Ark of the Covenant side by side with the whole ones? Brachot 8b

The verse quoted above from the Talmud refers to the story in the Torah when Moshe first smashes the Ten Commandments after seeing that the Israelites built the Golden Calf, but then gets a second set of Tablets, both the whole tablets and the smashed ones are placed in the ark of the Covenant.

- Why do you think that is? What does that say about us as human beings?

DEFINING ELDERLY: PERSPECTIVES ON HIDDUR P'NAI ZAKEN

Read the following text from Vayikra 19:32. What does the text instruct us to do? Why do you think it gives these instructions?

מִפְּנֵי שֵׂיבָה תָּקוּם וְהָדַרְתָּ פְּנֵי זָקֵן וְיָרֵאתָ מֵּאֱלֹהֶיךָ אֲנִי יְהוָה׃

You shall rise before the aged (seva) *and show deference to the old* (zaken); *You shall fear your God: I am Adonai.* Vayikra 19:32

- Does it make sense for us today to rise before the old?
- If we did, what would we be saying about our attitudes toward the elderly?
- Do you think that there is a difference between the old (*zaken*) and the aged (*sevah*)?
- How do the two parts of the sentence fit together?
- What connection could there be between honoring an old man and... fearing God?

הוא היה אומר בן ששים לזקנה. בן שבעים לשיבה. בן שמונים לגבורה. בן תשעים לשוח. בן מאה כאלו מת ועבר ובטל מן העולם:

He [Judah ben Tema] used to say: "At sixty a man attains old age (ziknah)*, at seventy he attains white old age* (sevah)*, at eighty "strength", at ninety a bent back, at one hundred as if he were dead and gone from the world. Avot 5:24*

- According to this text, what is the difference between *ziknah* and *sevah*?

We now have an insight into the Jewish attitude towards the aged; a *zaken* is deserving of honor no matter what his scholarly accomplishments have been. As much as we are to show respect for one who has acquired Torah, an old man is to be honored even if he has not acquired knowledge of the Torah. But why should this be so? When we honor one who has acquired much knowledge of the Torah, it is not the person himself we are honoring, but rather the Torah that he embodies.

- Why then must we honor the physical presence of the *zaken*?
- What is there about a *zaken* that commands the respect that we are supposed to show him?

HIDDUR P'NAI ZAKEN

Then...

Before answering these questions, it is necessary that we reflect upon the way in which *zekenim* were treated in Talmudic and Medieval times. In the first place, there simply were not many people alive in any one generation who reached what we would call "old age." Life expectancy was perhaps 40 or 50 years at most. It was unusual for one to live to the age of *zikna* (defined in the Talmud as being a minimum of 60 years). People looked up to the aged in the hope that they too would be blessed with such a long life. Who, indeed, would not have stood in awe as a person who had reached the age of *zikna* (60) or *seva* (70) entered a room! In traditional societies respect for elders was a virtue inculcated into children from infancy. Bestowing honor on elders (*zekenim* as well as parents) was a commandment that needed little rationale from Maimonides' time until modern times.

And now...

In modern society respect for the aged does not come quite so automatically. It is no longer unusual for a person to be alive and mobile at the age of 80 or even 90. The achievement of age no longer possesses the almost mystical aura that it once had. Moreover, old people at the ages of *zikna* and *seva* are far more common now than ever before. Perhaps modern people have become desensitized to the wonder of old age. We take old age for granted: it is no longer a goal to pray for, but an inevitability to be postponed for as long as possible.

Today people age 70 and up are living rich, full lives. The internet, telephones and e-mail all help to allow even those people who are homebound to keep up with the outside world on a moment to moment basis.

EXERCISE: DEFINING ELDERLY

List the names of some elderly people with whom you are acquainted. Briefly describe them—how they look, what they do, etc.

1. Name____Age__________

Relationship to you______________________Description____________________

____

____

2. Name____Age__________

Relationship to you______________________Description____________________

____

____

- ➢ How many of your elderly acquaintances are over 70?
- ➢ Do you consider people over 60 to be elderly? Are your grandparents elderly?

It used to be that people did not live as long on the average as we do today. A person who was fortunate to live to be 60 or 70 was quite a rarity.

- ➢ Do we consider it unusual for people to live to be 60 or 70?
- ➢ What is an age we might consider to be unusually old?
- ➢ How should we define the group of people we call "elderly"?

The rather arbitrary grouping "over 65" includes the widest variety of people. There are the "young" elderly—a great many of whom work, do extensive volunteer service, travel and live as actively when they were "young"—and there are the physically infirm who cannot work or move around easily, and who are often isolated in their homes or confined to nursing homes. As with any other age group, there is a wide diversity in health education, housing, income, religious attitudes and behavior, mental outlook, family status and geographical location.

Respect for the elderly that we learn from Vayikra 19:32 teaches us the idea to "Honor Your Mother and Father."

- ➢ How might these two ideas be related? In earlier times, when people died at earlier ages, old age came on at a relatively earlier time than today.
- ➢ Do you consider your parents to be elderly?

- How is the respect that you give to your parents different from the respect demanded in Vayikra for the elderly? How is it the same?
- What do you think are the characteristics of being parents and of being old that are the same?

Hiddur P'nai Zaken in North American History

It is clear from the early history of the synagogue that it has been a unique institution – it served as the hub of the community, and the focus for carrying out the mitzvot enumerated in the Mishnah Peah excerpted above. Special groups were organized through the synagogue with such titles as "Upbringers of Orphans," "Clothers of the Naked," "Crown of the Aged," "Comforters of Mourners" and so on. There were voluntary associations of lay persons whose participation was inspired both by the Law and their association with the synagogue-community. In the middle ages, the elderly in need of care may have been cared for in shelters for the sick or in places for the homeless (*hekdesh*). The need for treating the aged as a separate group apart from the sick and the poor did not come until modern times, as industrialization and urbanization disrupted and estranged families. Societies for the aging and homes for aged grew up during the nineteenth century and in America proliferated with the massive Eastern European migration—and the resultant disruptions of family life.

The sponsorship of philanthropy also came from many concerned, non-observant Jews, and thus many of the social services established for new immigrants and the aged were organized by Jews out of a traditional notion of obligation, but without direct reference to either the Law or the synagogue. Urbanization encouraged the centralization of aged care, and the professionalization of social work contributed to the separation of the synagogue and social service agencies. By 1930, the separation was virtually complete. Prior to 1900, there were only nine Jewish homes for the aged; today there are homes in virtually every major Jewish community.

As a result of the centralization, professionalization and transience of modern American society, the synagogue has been weakened as an institution. The requirements of centralization not only of social services, but of fund-raising and education, have lessened reliance on the synagogue for providing community leadership; the professionalization of life, including the functions within the synagogue, have lessened attendance and participation in the regular observances of Judaism; and transience which restricts the time and motivation to sink roots has attenuated loyalties between families and local institutions. These trends have radically altered the societal framework and the attitudinal structure through which the modern Jew deals with his aging relatives and with his own aging process. Ironically, these societal trends have in turn increased the consciousness of a need for stronger local institutions and thus a greater role in the local synagogue.
A Guide to Aging Programs for Synagogues , New York: Synagogue Council of America, 1975, pp.9-10

As much as synagogues and communities today have a renewed responsibility toward the elderly, so too must each individual undertake action to help the aged.

- What role can you play in taking responsibility toward the elderly?

The needs of the elderly are constantly changed by the multiple losses of role, status, income and health. They are further affected by the loss of spouse, family, neighbors and friends through death or migration. An older person may find himself isolated at a time when the emotional support of others is needed. Fear, loneliness and enforced inactivity reduce participation in community life and increase isolation. Caught in this cycle, and unaware of existing community services which are available to help, these people are the most difficult to identify and often the most needy.

EXERCISE: Understanding the Needs of the Elderly

What are some needs and desires of the elderly people that you mentioned on page 46?

1.____

2..____

3..____

4 .____

5.____.

- ➢ Which of these needs can be satisfied by individuals like you? How?
- ➢ Which of these needs can be satisfied by the Jewish community? How?
- ➢ Which of these needs may not be able to be satisfied at all? Why?
- ➢ Where are there places in your individual communities where you think that you might be able to make a difference with the elderly?

TRADITION TEACHES US ABOUT OLD AGE

In Jewish tradition it is not only said that we must honor our elders, but that it is an honor to achieve a ripe old age. Advanced years in themselves are not an honor, but when achieved "in the way of righteousness," then they are considered to be wearing "a crown of glory." (Mishlei 16:31).

The Bible emphasizes the inter-relationship between the way in which we live our lives, and the nature of the "harvest" of old age. The Fifth commandment states: "Honor your father and mother, that your days may be long in the land that the Lord your God gives to you." And the belief that longevity is the reward for a good life is summed up in Jacob's response to the Pharoah's question asking Jacob's age. He answered: "The days of the years of my sojournings are a hundred and thirty years; few and evil have been the days of the years of my life, and they have not attained unto the days of the years of the life of my fathers in the days of their sojournings." (Bereshit 47:9)

The rabbinic literature offers a poignant counterpoint between the growth in wisdom and learning that is achievable only with age, and the physical decline characteristic of old age.

> "He who learns from the young, eats unripe grapes and drinks new wine," it is stated in the Talmud; while "he who learns from the old eats ripe grapes and drinks old wine." Another rabbinic sage advised: "If the old say 'tear down' and the children 'build' – then you should tear down, for the 'destruction' of the old is construction; the 'construction' of the young, 'destruction." As for the physical realities, the unattractiveness of old age is treated metaphorically: "Youth is a crown of roses; old age a crown of (heavy) willows;" and practically: a man must pray that in his later years, "his eyes may see, his mouth eat, his legs walk, for in old age all powers fail."
>
> According to the rabbis too, oldness itself is not a virtue; wisdom and knowledge of Torah determine its value. The truly successful life is one which goes on growing and developing to the very end, which reaches its last day with full mental and physical powers. (Deut. 34:7). A Guide to Aging Programs for Synagogues , pp. 5-9

וְאַתָּה תָּבוֹא אֶל־אֲבֹתֶיךָ בְּשָׁלוֹם תִּקָּבֵר בְּשֵׂיבָה טוֹבָה׃

(God said to Abram), "You shall go to your fathers in peace; you shall be buried at a ripe old age."
Bereshit 15:15

לֹא־יִהְיֶה מִשָּׁם עוֹד עוּל יָמִים וְזָקֵן אֲשֶׁר לֹא־יְמַלֵּא
אֶת־יָמָיו כִּי הַנַּעַר בֶּן־מֵאָה שָׁנָה יָמוּת וְהַחוֹטֶא בֶּן־מֵאָה שָׁנָה יְקֻלָּל׃

No more shall there be an infant or a graybeard who does not live out his days. He who dies at a hundred years shall be reckoned a youth, and he who failed to reach a hundred shall be reckoned accursed. Isaiah 65:20

כַּבֵּד אֶת־אָבִיךָ וְאֶת־אִמֶּךָ לְמַעַן יַאֲרִכוּן יָמֶיךָ
עַל הָאֲדָמָה אֲשֶׁר־יְהוָה אֱלֹהֶיךָ נֹתֵן לָךְ׃

Honor your father and mother that your days may be long upon the land that the Lord your God gives you. Shemot 20:12

Compare this verse from Shemot 20:12 to the verse in Vayikra 19:32 found on page 44. Are the two related?

CONTRASTING TEXTS

Read the following texts and consider what they mean to you.

בִּישִׁישִׁים חָכְמָה וְאֹרֶךְ יָמִים תְּבוּנָה׃

With aged men is wisdom; And length of day brings understanding. Job 12:12

לֹא־רַבִּים יֶחְכָּמוּ וּזְקֵנִים יָבִינוּ מִשְׁפָּט׃

The old are not always wise; Nor do the aged understand judgment. Job 32:9

- How could the author of the Book of Job believe in both of these ideas? Don't they contradict one another?

> אין מושיבין בסנהדרי אלא בעלי קומה, ובעלי חכמה, ובעלי מראה, ובעלי זקנה,
>
> *None are to be appointed members of the Sanhedrin but men of stature, wisdom, good appearance, mature age...* Sanhedrin 17a

- Why is each one of these things important?
- What if a person has some qualities, but not the others?

> אין מושיבין בסנהדרין זקן וסריס ומי שאין לו בנים רבי יהודה מוסיף: אף אכזרי.
>
> *We do not appoint as members of the Sanhedrin an aged man, a eunuch, or one who is childless. Rabbi Judah added: a cruel man.* Sanhedrin 36b

- Don't these two verses also contradict each other?
- How can the two descriptions of the Sanhedrin members both be in the Talmud?
- How might each verse refer to different situations or circumstances?
- Why does Jewish tradition have differing opinions toward treatment of the elderly?

We now have an insight into the Jewish attitude towards the aged; a *zaken* is deserving of honor no matter what his scholarly accomplishments have been. As much as we are to show respect for one who has acquired Torah, an old man is to be honored even if he has not acquired knowledge of the Torah. But why should this be so? When we honor one who has acquired much knowledge of the Torah, it is not the person himself we are honoring, but rather the Torah that he embodies.

- Why then must we honor the physical presence of the *zaken*?
- What is there about a *zaken* that commands the respect that we are supposed to show him?

Now read the next two texts from Kiddishin and Sefer HaChinuch and think about the following questions:

- What do the elderly possess that should entitle them to the respect of younger people?
- Do you agree with Issi ben Yehuda when he says that we should rise before the aged, regardless of whether or not they are learned in the Torah?
- What do all elderly people have, according to Issi ben Yehuda?

ת"ר: (ויקרא יט) מפני שיבה תקום - יכול אפילו מפני זקן
אשמאי? ת"ל: זקן, ואין זקן אלא חכם, שנאמר: (במדבר יא) אספה לי
שבעים איש מזקני ישראל - רבי יוסי הגלילי אומר: אין זקן אלא מי שקנה חכמה,
שנאמר: (משלי ח) ה' קנני ראשית דרכו.
איסי בן יהודה אומר: מפני שיבה תקום - אפילו כל שיבה במשמע.

Our Rabbis taught: "You shall rise before the aged and show deference to the old; you shall fear your God: I am the Lord" (Vayikra 19:32). You might think one must honor even a wicked old man. But the Torah used the word zaken (elder) which means "wise man", as it says, "Gather for Me seventy men from the elders of Israel, whom you know to be elders and officers of the people, and bring them to the Tent of Meeting and let them take their place with you" (Bamidbar 11:16). [In this sense, elders take on a connotation of more than just "old men".] R. Yose the Galilean says zaken (an 'elder') is only one who acquired wisdom, as it says, "The Lord made me (kanani) as the beginning of His way" [Proverb 8:22 – based on a play on the Hebrew word "kanani"] ...Issi ben Yehuda says, "You shall rise before the aged. This means that all old men (whether they are wise or not) are included."
Kiddushin 32b

- Does this mean that elders are always right?
- What is the text trying to teach regarding the relationship of elders and young people?

Honor of the wise:
One of the rationales for this mitzvah is that the essence of man in this world is to acquire more and more wisdom in order to know his Creator. Therefore it is fitting to honor one who has attained wisdom, so that others will be encouraged to do the same. And for this reason, Issi ben Yehuda said in the Gemara (Kiddushin 32b) that even a wicked old man [deserves honor]. That is, one who is not knowledgeable is included in the mitzvah of honoring the elderly, since during his many years he has come to recognize God's works and His wonders, and therefore he (the zaken) should be honored. And this agrees with what R. Yohanan said, that the law is according to Issi ben Yehuda; "As long as the old person is not a blatant sinner; because if so, he prevents himself from being honored."
Sefer HaHinuch, No. 257

- What does this selection from Sefer HaChinuch add to the text from the Talmud in Kiddushin 32b?
- Does anything we have read in Job or Sanhedrin modify in any way the ideas found in Vayikra, Kiddushin or Sefer HaChinuch—that the elderly deserve respect because they are wise in their own experience?

WHAT HAPPENS TO THE ELDERLY

...when they can no longer work?

וַיְדַבֵּר יְהוָה אֶל־מֹשֶׁה לֵּאמֹר׃ זֹאת אֲשֶׁר לַלְוִיִּם מִבֶּן חָמֵשׁ וְעֶשְׂרִים שָׁנָה וָמַעְלָה יָבוֹא לִצְבֹא צָבָא בַּעֲבֹדַת אֹהֶל מוֹעֵד׃ וּמִבֶּן חֲמִשִּׁים שָׁנָה יָשׁוּב מִצְּבָא הָעֲבֹדָה וְלֹא יַעֲבֹד עוֹד׃ וְשֵׁרֵת אֶת־אֶחָיו בְּאֹהֶל מוֹעֵד לִשְׁמֹר מִשְׁמֶרֶת וַעֲבֹדָה לֹא יַעֲבֹד כָּכָה תַּעֲשֶׂה לַלְוִיִּם בְּמִשְׁמְרֹתָם׃

The Lord spoke to Moses saying, "This is the rule for the Levites; from 25 years of age up they shall participate in the work force in the service of the Tent of Meeting but at age 50 they shall retire from the work force and shall serve no more. They may assist their brother Levites at the Tent of Meeting by standing guard, but they shall perform no labor. Thus you shall deal with the Levites with regard to their duties." Bamidbar 8:23-26

...when they are physically weak and cannot take care of themselves?

אַל־תַּשְׁלִיכֵנִי לְעֵת זִקְנָה כִּכְלוֹת כֹּחִי אַל־תַּעַזְבֵנִי׃

Do not cast me off in time of old age; Forsake me not when my strength is spent. Tehillim 71:9

צריך אדם להתפלל על זקנתו שתהא עיניו רואות ופיו אוכל ורגליו מהלכות שבזמן שאדם יזקין הכל מסתלק ממנו

A person must pray concerning his old age that his eyes see, his mouth eat, and his legs walk, for in old age these abilities depart. Tanhuma, Mikketz 10

...when they are mentally incapacitated and are easily confused and forgetful?

והלומד זקן למה הוא דומה. לדיו כתובה על ניר מחוק.

What does learning when old resemble? It is like writing on blotted paper. Avot 4:25

...when they are defenseless against the cruelty of others?

הָעָם אִישׁ בְּאִישׁ וְאִישׁ בְּרֵעֵהוּ יִרְהֲבוּ הַנַּעַר בַּזָּקֵן וְהַנִּקְלֶה בַּנִּכְבָּד׃

So the people shall oppress one another—Each oppressing his fellow:
The young shall bully the old, and the despised shall bully the honored. Isaiah 3:5

...when they fear the end of life and the insecurities of the future?

שְׂמַח בָּחוּר בְּיַלְדוּתֶיךָ וִיטִיבְךָ לִבְּךָ בִּימֵי בְחוּרוֹתֶךָ וְהַלֵּךְ בְּדַרְכֵי לִבְּךָ וּבְמַרְאֵי עֵינֶיךָ.

Rejoice, O young man, in your youth, and be happy in the days of your youth, and walk in the ways of your heart, and in the sight of your eyes... Kohelet 11:9

כשאדם נער אומר דברי זמר, הגדיל אומר דברי משלות, הזקין אומר דברי הבלים.

When a man is young he quotes poetry; when he matures, he quotes proverbs; when he is old, he speaks of futilities. **Shir HaShirim Rabbah 1:10**

We can now try to understand why any *zaken* is deserving of honor.

HOW DO WE ANSWER THESE QUESTIONS?

- Today, there are more opportunities for the elderly then ever before. What are some things that you do, which you think that elderly people can not do?
- Should age be a hindrance for someone who wants to skydive, or to play basketball, or to work in a full time position?

A NEW CHALLENGE: ALZHEIMER'S DISEASE

Alzheimer's is a disease that primarily affects the elderly and causes the loss of basic memory functions.

- How do you think it would feel to visit a close relative who no longer recognizes you?
- Does your visit matter if they won't remember that you were there?

Read the story below. Did you ever think that there would be someone at 87 years old who would want to do the things that Martha did?

Tap Dancing with Martha

Why not? The story goes that a number of residents of a nursing home were coming back from a show when one of them, Martha Colcord (87 years old at the time), told her program supervisor, Neila Houghton-Daggett, that she'd really like to learn how to tap dance.

Ms. Houghton-Daggett must have thought to herself, "Why not?" So, she got Ms. Colcord a teacher.

And then she wanted to ride a motorcycle. And Ms. Houghton-Daggett must have thought, "Why not?" And then Ms. Colcord wanted to ride in a helicopter.

And Ms. Houghton-Daggett must have thought, "Well, why not?"

Horseback riding. Sure.

Everything but parachuting and hang-gliding. But some of them did manage to do a round of hot air ballooning.

Now, if we had a few thousand more Neila Houghton-Daggetts around in nursing homes everywhere, the cumulative added happy years of the lives of residents in nursing homes would certainly reach several million.

Why not?

And as best as I can tell from meeting Ms. Houghton-Daggett and Ms. Colcord, the former never said to the latter, "You're too old to do that!" or "You're not well enough to do that!" or "Our lawyers say we can't do that because of liability problems!"

And the word from Ms. Houghton-Daggett is that someone else like her in another nursing home Somewhere Out There arranged a hotel and transportation and a travel partner for a woman 107 years old who always wanted to see a Macy's Thanksgiving Day Parade. Why not?

Heroes and Miracle Workers by Danny Siegel

- What are your reactions to this true story?
- Do you know any older people who are still active in their 80's and 90's?
- How can you help elderly people to achieve their reams at an old age?

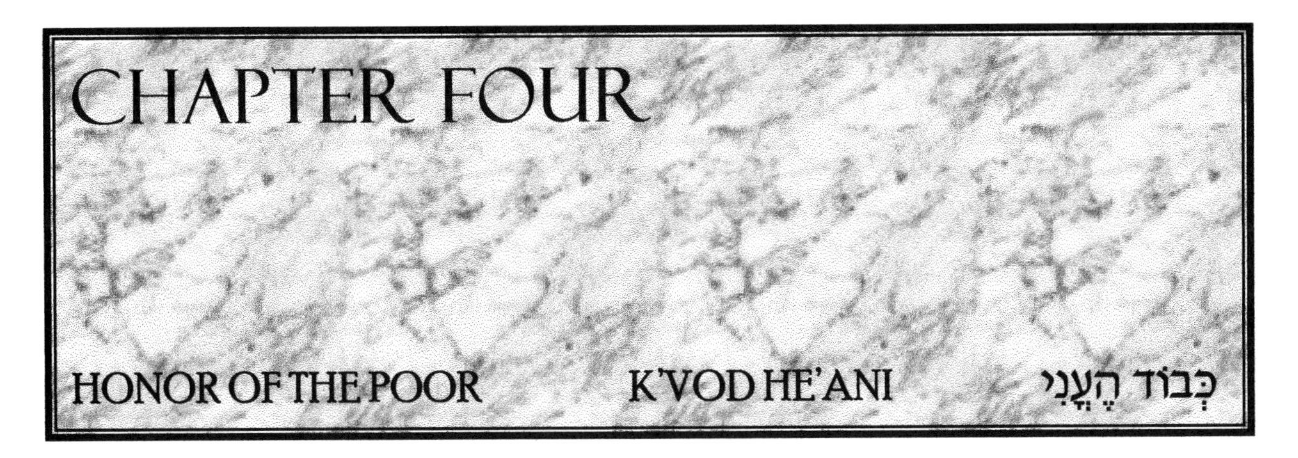

א"ר יונה אשרי נותן לדל אין כתיב כאן אלא אשרי משכיל אל דל הדא דמסתכל במצוה.

Rabbi Yonah said:
The verse doesn't say "Happy are those who give to the poor," but rather, "Happy are the ones who use their insight when giving to the poor," (Tehillim 41:2) *meaning, those who use all their faculties when considering how to do the mitzvah of tzedakah.* Talmud Yerushalmi, Pe'ah 37b

Giving money to charity seems like a simple task. We are frequently offered opportunities to contribute to numerous funds. Dedicated volunteers solicit our donations to their favorite causes in shopping centers and supermarkets; cyclists and joggers ask for our support in bike and walk-a-thons; charity boxes face us in restaurants and schools. If we give small change whenever we are confronted with the opportunity to give, we might well feel that we have fulfilled a basic human obligation to share with those who are less fortunate than ourselves.

Doing an act of tzedakah, however, is a more difficult task. As previously discussed in the introduction to this sourcebook, Tzedakah not only means "giving money to charity"; tzedakah also means giving with sensitivity to those who need, and giving because sharing is the just and proper way for us to behave. Consideration of these questions has become the foundation of Jewish sensitivities toward the poor:

- How to collect tzedakah
- How to distribute tzedakah
- The attitude of the donor toward the recipient and the recipient toward the donor
- How much is a proper contribution
- Do needy people always only need money? What else might they be in need of?

CONSIDER TZEDAKAH

- Do you feel obligated to give tzedakah?
- Have you ever not wanted to give tzedakah? Why?
- What are the reasons to contribute to tzedakah?
- What might prevent you from contributing?

EXERCISE: Why Give Tzedakah

Do you agree with the following texts? Circle your answer! Be ready to support your decision!

אפי' עני המתפרנס מן הצדקה יעשה צדקה.

Even a poor person who receives tzedakah must give from what he receives. *Gittin 7b*

AGREE **DISAGREE**

אם רואה אדם שמזונותיו מצומצמין יעשה מהן צדקה, וכ"ש כשהן מרובין.

If a person sees that his resources are limited, let him use them for tzedakah—and so much the more so if he has extensive resources. *Gittin 7a*

AGREE **DISAGREE**

אין מחשבין בצדקה עם גבאי צדקה, ולא בהקדש עם הגזברין.

He who causes others to give tzedakah is greater than the giver himself. *Baba Batra 9a*

AGREE **DISAGREE**

אמרו עליו על בנימין הצדיק שהיה ממונה על קופה של צדקה,
פעם אחת באתה אשה לפניו בשני בצורת, אמרה לו: רבי, פרנסני אמר לה:
העבודה, שאין בקופה של צדקה כלום אמרה לו: רבי, אם אין אתה מפרנסני, הרי
אשה ושבעה בניה מתים עמד ופרנסה משלו.

A story is told of Binyamin HaTzaddik who was the supervisor of the community's tzedakah funds. Once, when food was scarce, a woman came to him and said, "Rabbi, feed me!" He replied, "I swear there is nothing in the tzedakah fund." She said, "If you do not feed me, a woman and her seven children will die." So he fed her from his own money. Baba Batra 11a

AGREE **DISAGREE**

COLLECTING AND DISTRIBUTING TZEDAKAH

Kevod HeAni is such a multi-faceted mitzvah. There are so many components of the mitzvah, that sometimes it is overwhelming to be able to make sense of them. Judaism speaks individually about collecting and distributing tzedakah, the obligation to give tzedakah, who should receive tzedakah, how to give tzedakah, giving tzedakah as a community, and even how much to give.

תנו רבנן: קופה של צדקה נגבית בשנים ומתחלקת בשלשה, נגבית בשנים - שאין עושים שררות על הצבור פחות משנים, ומתחלקת בשלשה - כדיני ממונות.

Our Rabbis taught: The charity fund is collected by two persons (jointly) and distributed by three. It is collected by two, because any office conferring authority over the community must be filled by at least two persons. It must be distributed by three, on the analogy of money cases [which are handled by a court of three] **Baba Batra 8b**

תמחוי נגבית בשלשה ומתחלקת בשלשה, שגבויה וחלוקה שוים. תמחוי - בכל יום, קופה - מערב שבת לערב שבת.

Food for the soup kitchen is collected by three and distributed by three, since it is distributed as soon as it is collected. Food is distributed every day, the monetary (tzedakah) fund every Friday.
Baba Batra 8b

ת"ר: גבאי צדקה אינן רשאין לפרוש זה מזה, אבל פורש זה לשער וזה לחנות מצא מעות בשוק - לא יתנם בתוך כיסו, אלא נותנן לתוך ארנקי של צדקה, ולכשיבא לביתו יטלם כיוצא בו.

Our Rabbis taught: The collectors of charity (when collecting) are not permitted to separate from one another, though one may collect at the gate while the other collects at a shop in the same courtyard. If one of them finds money in the street, he should not put it in his purse but into the tzedakah box, and take it out again when he comes home. Baba Batra 8b

תנו רבנן: גבאי צדקה שאין להם עניים לחלק - פורטין לאחרים ואין פורטין לעצמן גבאי תמחוי שאין להם עניים לחלק - מוכרין לאחרים ואין מוכרין לעצמן מעות של צדקה אין מונין אותן שתים, אלא אחת אחת.

Our Rabbis taught: If the collectors (still have money but) no poor to whom to distribute it, they should change the small coins into larger ones with other persons, but not from their own money. If the stewards of the soup kitchen (have food left over and) no poor to whom to distribute it, they may sell it to others but not to themselves. In counting out the money collected for tzedakah, they should not count the coins two at a time, but only one at a time. **Baba Batra 8b**

- To whom do these texts show sensitivity?
- To whom do they show insensititivity?
- What do these texts teach about giving tzedakah?
- What specific tzedakah-giving procedure do these text address?

- How do you feel about the message of the texts?
- Is it still a valid message today?

EXERCISE: WHO SHOULD RECEIVE MY TZEDAKAH?

Read the following text and then fill in the concentric circles according to the priorities of tzedakah in your text. (An example has been given for you to begin.)

יש לו לאדם, מזונות הרבה בתוך ביתו, ובקש לעשות מהן צדקה כדי שיפרנס אחרים, כאי זה צד יעשה, יפרנס את אביו ואת אמו תחילה, ואם הותיר יפרנס את אחיו ואת אחותו, ואם הותיר יפרנס את בני ביתו, ואם הותיר יפרנס את בני משפחתו, ואם הותיר יפרנס את בני שכונתו, ואם הותיר יפרנס את בני מבוי, מיכן ואילך ירבה צדקה בישראל.

If a person has food in his home and wishes to perform an act of tzedakah with it, first he must sustain his father and mother; if there is any (food) remaining, he should sustain his brothers and sisters; after that, the other members of his household; after that, other members of his family; after that, those who dwell in his immediate area; after that, those who dwell in his neighborhood; from then on, he may increase his benevolence among the Jewish people. Seder Eliyahu Rabbah (27) 25

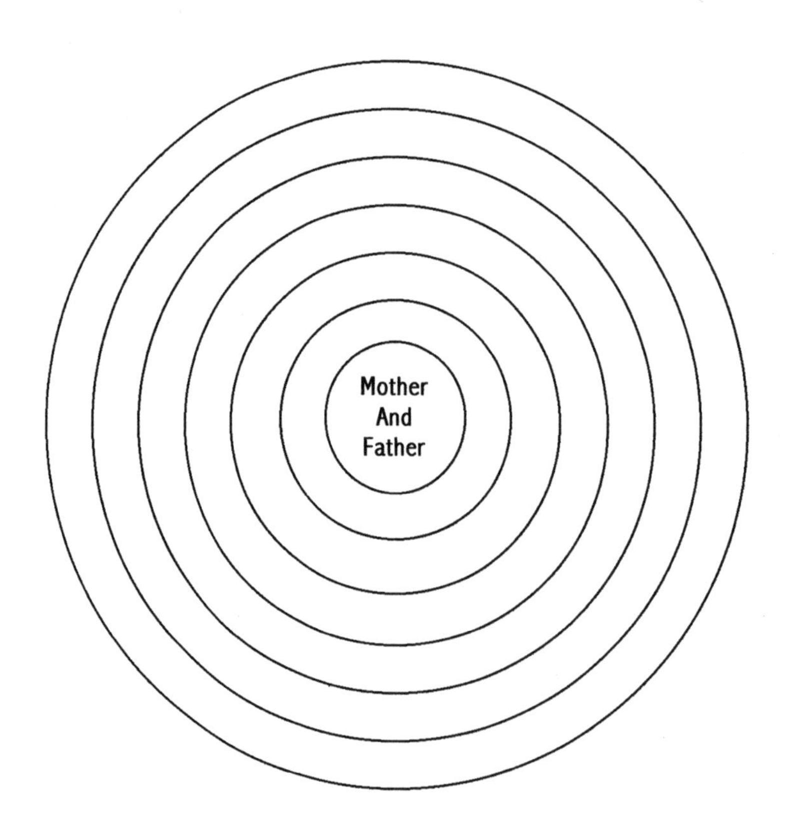

- Where do you think that non-Jews should fit on these circles?
- Should Jews give tzedakah to non-Jews? Why?

Look at your answers to the questions on the previous page. Are your answers reflected in the following Jewish texts about who should receive?

ת"ר: יתום ויתומה
שבאו להתפרנס, מפרנסין את היתומה ואחר כך מפרנסין את היתום, מפני
שהאיש דרכו לחזור על הפתחים, ואין אשה דרכה לחזור. יתום ויתומה
שבאו לינשא, משיאין את היתומה ואחר כך משיאין את היתום, מפני
שבושתה של אשה מרובה משל איש.

Our Rabbis taught: If an orphan boy and an orphan girl applied for maintenance, the girl orphan is to be maintained first and the boy orphan afterwards, because it is not unusual for a man to go begging but it is unusual for a woman to do so. If an orphan boy and orphan girl come to be married, we enable the girl to marry first, and afterward enable the boy to marry, because the shame of a woman is greater than that of a man Kebubot 67a-67b

ת"ר: המסמא את עינו, והמצבה את בטנו, והמקפח את שוקו - אינו נפטר מן העולם
עד שיבא לידי כך. המקבל צדקה ואין צריך לכך, סופו אינו נפטר מן העולם עד
שיבא לידי כך.

Our Rabbis taught: If a man pretends to have a blind eye, a swollen belly, or a shrunken leg, he will not pass out from the world before actually coming into such a condition. If a man accepts charity and is not in need of it his end (will be that) he will not pass out of the world before he comes to such a condition (i.e. needing tzedakah) Kebubot 68a

EXERCISE: Placing Priority

If you had to decide the best way to give tzedakah, could you? Write your own levels of giving tzedakah from the most selfless way to the most selfish way.

MOST SELFLESS ____________________________

____

____

____

____

MOST SELFISH ____________________________

- What are the most important ways that you can give tzedakah?

DEVELOPING TZEDAKAH PRIORITIES

FYI:
Moses ben Maimon (1135-1204), a rabbinic authority of Spanish birth, codifier, philosopher, and royal physician, is known in Rabbinic literature as "**Rambam**" from the acronym **R**abbi **M**oses **B**en **M**aimon. He spent ten years writing the *Mishneh Torah*, a codification of the Oral Law, from which he believed all Jews could systematically learn (in his words) the correct way to determine what was forbidden and permitted, as well as other laws of the Torah. The task of the *Mishnah Torah* was to present the results of Rambam's own study of the literature written by the Rabbis in talmudic times in such a way that everyone, and not only scholars, could understand what behaviors were required of them. The *Mishneh Torah* is divided into 14 books, each representing a distinct category of the Jewish legal system.

Maimonides developed the following priority order for giving tzedakah with the intention of preserving the dignity of the recipient. He recognized that a challenge exists for both the giver and the receiver and tried to make the process as easy as possible. Maimonides took the approach that it is better to give grudgingly rather than not at all, but makes it clear that the highest level of tzedakah is when the recipients are given a skill to earn their own money and never have to ask for money again. The selection below is excerpted from the section of the *Mishneh Torah* entitled "Hilchot Matanot Aniyyim" – "Laws of Gifts for the Poor," 10:7-14

MAIMONIDES' LADDER OF TZEDAKAH
(in descending order)

ז שמנה מעלות יש בצדקה זו למעלה
מזו. מעלה גדולה שאין למעלה ממנה זה המחזיק ביד ישראל שמך ונותן לו
מתנה או הלואה או עושה עמו שותפות או ממציא לו מלאכה כדי לחזק את ידו
עד שלא יצטרך לבריות לשאול. ועל זה נאמר והחזקת בו גר ותושב וחי עמך
כלומר החזק בו עד שלא יפול ויצטרך.

ח פחות מזה הנותן צדקה לעניים ולא
ידע למי נתן ולא ידע העני ממי לקח, שהרי זו מצוה לשמה, כגון לשכת
חשאים שהיתה במקדש, שהיו הצדיקים נותנין בה בחשאי והעניים בני טובים
מתפרנסין ממנה בחשאי, וקרוב לזה הנותן לתוך קופה של צדקה, ולא יתן
אדם לתוך קופה של צדקה אלא אם כן יודע שהממונה נאמן וחכם ויודע
להנהיג כשורה כר׳ חנניה בן תרדיון.

ט פחות מזה שידע הנותן למי יתן ולא
ידע העני ממי לקח, כגון גדולי החכמים שהיו הולכין בסתר ומשליכין המעות
בפתחי העניים, וכזה ראוי לעשות ומעלה טובה היא אם אין הממונין בצדקה נוהגין כשורה.

י פחות מזה שידע העני ממי נטל ולא ידע הנותן, כגון גדולי
החכמים שהיו צוררים המעות בסדיניהן ומפשילין לאחוריהן ובאין העניים
ונוטלין כדי שלא יהיה להן בושה.

יא פחות מזה שיתן לו בידו קודם שישאל.

יב פחות מזה שיתן לו אחר שישאל.

יג פחות מזה שיתן לו פחות מן הראוי בסבר פנים יפות.

יד פחות מזה שיתן לו בעצב.

1) A gift, a loan, a business partnership, a job rendering alms unnecessary…

2) Benevolence in which the giver and the recipients are unknown to each other…Similar to this is one who puts money into the communal tzedakah box…

3) Benevolence in which the giver is unknown to the recipient (but the recipient is known to the giver)…

4) Benevolence in which the recipient is unknown to the giver (but the giver is known to the recipient)…

5) Giving before one is asked to give.

6) Giving after one is asked to give.

7) Giving less than appropriate, but graciously.

8) Giving grudgingly.

- How does the list of Maimonides compare to your list?
- Why do you think that Maimonides chose that order?

HOW TO GIVE TZEDAKAH

Giving money is not always just as simple as putting money in a tzedakah box.

- What are some ways that you think you can give money to someone who needs it besides putting money in a tzedakah box or handing a person some change on the street?
- Can you think of ways to give that would allow the recipient to keep his/her dignity?
- Can you think of ways of giving that would be appropriate?

EXERCISE: Maimondes Match-Up

Each of the following texts demonstrates a way of giving tzedakah according to Maimonides' Ladder of Tzedakah. Using what you have learned, try to match up the text with the correct ladder step. (Please note that not every step is represented.)

...לשכת חשאים יראי חטא נותנים לתוכה בחשאי, ועניים בני טובים מתפרנסים מתוכה בחשאי.

…[T]here was a secret chamber in the Temple where pious people would leave money in secret, and those who had been well-to-do but had become poor would come and take in secret.
Mishnah Shekalim 5:6

Level of Tzedakah:_______

פתוח תפתח. נתון תתן. למה נאמר כולם מגיד הכתוב הראוי ליתן לו פת נותנים לו פת הראוי ליתן לו עיסה נותנים לו עיסה הראוי ליתן לו מעה נותנים לו מעה הראוי להאכילו בתוך פיו מאכילים אותו בתוך פיו:

"You shall open [your hand] wide [to your brother, to the poor, to the needy]" (Devarim 15:11). *Why are all (three) stated? To him for whom bread is suitable give bread; to him who needs dough, give dough; to him for whom money is required, give money; to him for whom it is fitting to put the food in his mouth, put it into his mouth.* Sifre Devarim Re'eh, 118

Level of Tzedakah:_______

תנא: אם היה מחזיר על הפתחים - אין נזקקין לו. ההוא עניא דהוה מחזיר על הפתחים דאתא לקמיה דרב פפא, לא מזדקיק ליה. א"ל רב סמא בריה דרב ייבא לרב פפא: אי מר לא מזדקיק ליה, אינש אחרינא לא מזדקיק ליה, לימות ליה? והא תניא: אם היה עני המחזיר על הפתחים - אין נזקקין לו! א"ל: אין נזקקין לו למתנה מרובה, אבל נזקקין לו למתנה מועטת.

A Tanna taught: If he is a beggar who goes from door to door, we pay no attention to him. A certain man who used to beg from door to door came to Rav Papa (for money), but he ignored him. Rav Samma the son of Rav Yeva said to R. Papa, "If you do not pay attention to him, no one else will pay attention to him; is he then to die of hunger?" [R. Papa replied] "But has it not been taught, 'If he is a beggar who goes from door to door, we pay no attention to him'?" He replied, "We do not listen to his request for a large gift, but we do listen to his request for a small gift." Baba Batra 9a

Level of Tzedakah:_______

אמר רבי אבא אמר רבי שמעון בן לקיש:
גדול המלוה יותר מן העושה, צדקה, ומטיל בכיס יותר מכולן.

R. Abba said in the name of R. Shimon b. Lakish: "He who lends (money) is greater than he who performs charity; and he who forms a partnership is greater than all." Shabbat 63a

Level of Tzedakah:_______

ביתא דהוו בה שיתין אפייתא ביממא ושיתין אפייתא בליליא, ואפיין לכל מאן דצריך. ולא שקל ידא מן כיסא, דסבר: דילמא אתי עני בר טובים, ואדמטו ליה לכיסא קא מכסיף. ותו, הוו פתיחין ליה ארבע בבי לארבע רוחתא דעלמא, וכל דהוה עייל כפין נפיק כי שבע. והוו שדו ליה חטי ושערי בשני בצורת אבראי, דכל מאן דכסיפא מילתא למשקל ביממא אתי ושקיל בליליא.

[Rav. Hana b. Hanilai] had sixty bakers in his house day and night, baking for anyone who needed bread. He did not take his hand out of his pocket, so that when a person who had become poor came to ask, he would not feel humiliated [while Rav Hana went to get money for him]. His doors were open to all four directions, and anyone who came in hungry would leave satisfied. Furthermore, in times when food was scarce, he would leave wheat and barley outside the door so that anyone who was too embarrassed to come and take in the daytime could come unnoticed and take at night. Berachot 58b

Level of Tzedakah:_______

...וכמה עד חמישית נכסיו מצוה מן המובחר, ואחד מעשרה בנכסיו בינוני, פחות מכאן עין רעה

...[T]o give up to a fifth of one's wealth is the most preferable way to perform the mitzvah [of tzedakah]; to give one tenth of one's wealth is a middling way to perform it; to give less [than one tenth] is looked upon poorly. Mishneh Torah, Laws of Gifts for the Poor 7:5

Level of Tzedakah:________

EXERCISE: Developing Guidelines for Giving

Utilizing your experience from the collecting and distributing experiences and from discussing the texts from the Talmud, establish a list of guidelines that you consider to be the best ways for collecting and distributing Tzedakah money. When you have determined a number of guidelines, list them in priority order with number 1 as the most important and number 10 as the least important.

Collecting	Distributing
1.	1.
2.	2.
3.	3.
4.	4.
5.	5.
6.	6.
7.	7.
8.	8.
9.	9.
10.	10.

EXERCISE: Simulation Allocations Project

Allocating Tzedakah funds is not an easy process. There are so many organizations and people who are in need. How can you decide which is more important than another?

Read through the list of organizations in the Appendix on page 101. Think about how you would allocate money to the different agencies if you were on the allocations committee.

Now, decide how to rank the agencies that will receive the money. You would want to assign not a dollar value to each agency that asks for money, but rather a numeric system by which each agency is ranked in order of who would get the most money, down to who would get the least amount of money.

As you may have discovered, it is not an easy task to allocate money. Each of the organizations represented have valid and important reasons that they need the money. Every year, the International USY Social Action/Tikun Olam committee has a day that is dedicated to allocating all Tikun Olam funds that have not yet been allocated by USY chapters and regions.

א"ר יונה אשרי נותן לדל אין כתיב כאן אלא אשרי משכיל אל דל
הדא דמסתכל במצוה היאך לעשותה כיצד היה ר' יונה עושה כשהיה
רואה בן טובים שירד מנכסיו היה אומר לו בני בשביל ששמעתי שנפלה
לך ירושה ממקום אחר טול ואת פורע מן דהוה נסב ליה א"ל מתנה

R. Yonah said: It is not written, "Happy is he who gives to the poor," but "Happy is he who considers the poor" (Tehillim 41:2): *i.e., he who ponders how to fulfill the command to help the poor. How did R. Yonah act? If he met a man of good family, who had become impoverished, he would say, "Since I have heard that a legacy has been left to you from such a place, take this money in advance, and pay me back later." When the man accepted it, he then said to him, "It is a gift."* Jerusalem Talmud Pe'ah 37b

THINK ABOUT THIS!

מר עוקבא הוה עניא בשיבבותיה, דהוה רגיל כל יומא דשדי ליה ארבעה זוזי בצינורא דדשא.
יום אחד אמר: איזיל איחזי מאן קעביד בי ההוא טיבותא. ההוא יומא נגהא ליה למר עוקבא
לבי מדרשא, אתיא דביתהו בהדיה, כיון דחזיוה דקא מצלי ליה לדשא נפק בתרייהו, רהוט
מקמיה עיילי לההוא אתונא דהוה גרופה נורא, הוה קא מיקליין כרעיה דמר עוקבא, אמרה
ליה דביתהו: שקול כרעיך אותיב אכרעאי. חלש דעתיה, אמרה ליה: אנא שכיחנא בגויה
דביתא ומקרבא אהנייתי. ומאי כולי האי? דאמר מר זוטרא בר טוביה אמר רב, ואמרי לה
אמר רב הונא בר ביזנא אמר ר"ש חסידא, ואמרי לה א"ר יוחנן משום רבי שמעון בן יוחי:
נוח לו לאדם שימסור עצמו לתוך כבשן האש ואל ילבין פני חברו ברבים.

Mar Ukba had a poor man in his neighborhood into whose door-socket he used to throw four zuz [coins] every day. Once [the poor man] thought: "I will go and see who does this kindness for me." On that day [it happened] that Mar Ukba was late at the house of study and his wife was coming home with him. As soon as [the poor man] saw them moving the door he went out after them, but they fled from him and ran into a furnace from which the fire had just been swept. Mar Ukba's feet were burning and his wife said to him: "Raise your feet and put them on mine." Since he was upset [that he did not have the same divine protection as his wife], she said to him, "I am usually at home and my benefactions [for the poor] are direct." And what [was the reason for] all that? Because Mar Zutra b. Tobiah said in the name of Rav (Others state R. Huna b. Bizna said in the name of R. Simeon the Pious; and others again state: R. Johanan said in the name of R. Simeon b. Yohai): "Better had a man thrown himself into a fiery furnace then publicly embarrass his friend." Kebubot 67b

THE SILENT PUSHKE

Jewish families have traditionally given tzedakah by putting coins in the tzedakah box *("pushke")* in their homes on Friday evenings and holidays just before candles are lit. In addition, in order to mark special occasions such as births, bar/bat mitzvahs, and weddings, Jewish families donate money to appropriate tzedakot. Even on sad occasions when we pray for the recovery of someone seriously ill, or to honor the memory of someone who had died, it is a Jewish custom to contribute to tzedakah.

- ➢ Why is the *pushke* "silent"?
- ➢ What level of Maimonides' ladder is this?
- ➢ How does this relate to the passage from Ketubot above?

שבאו לינשא, משיאין את היתומה ואחר כך משיאין את היתום, מפני שבושתה של אשה
מרובה משל איש. ת"ר: יתום שבא לישא, שוכרין לו בית ומציעין לו מטה וכל כלי תשמישו,
ואחר כך משיאין לו אשה, שנאמר: (דברים ט"ו) די מחסורו אשר יחסר לו, די מחסורו
- זה הבית, אשר יחסר - זה מטה ושלחן, לו - זו אשה, וכן הוא אומר: (בראשית ב')
אעשה לו עזר כנגדו. תנו רבנן: די מחסורו - אתה מצווה עליו לפרנסו, ואי אתה מצווה עליו
לעשרו אשר יחסר לו - אפילו סוס לרכוב עליו ועבד לרוץ לפניו. אמרו עליו על הלל הזקן,
שלקח לעני בן טובים אחד סוס לרכוב עליו ועבד לרוץ לפניו פעם אחת לא מצא עבד
לרוץ לפניו, ורץ לפניו שלשה מילין. תנו רבנן: מעשה באנשי גליל העליון, שלקחו לעני בן
טובים אחד מציפורי ליטרא בשר בכל יום. ליטרא בשר מאי רבותא? אמר רב הונא: ליטרא
בשר משל עופות. ואיבעית אימא: בליטרא בשר ממש. רב אשי אמר: התם כפר קטן היה,
בכל יומא הוה מפסדי חיותא אמטולתיה. ההוא דאתא לקמיה דרבי נחמיה, אמר ליה: במה
אתה סועד? א"ל: בבשר שמן ויין ישן. רצונך שתגלגל עמי בעדשים? גלגל עמו בעדשים ומת,
אמר: אוי לו לזה שהרגו נחמיה אדרבה, אוי לו לנחמיה שהרגו לזה מיבעי ליה אלא, איהו
הוא דלא איבעי ליה לפנוקי נפשיה כולי האי. ההוא דאתא לקמיה דרבא, אמר לו: במה
אתה סועד? אמר לו: בתרנגולת פטומה ויין ישן. אמר ליה: ולא חיישת לדוחקא דציבורא?
א"ל: אטו מדידהו קאכילנא? מדרחמנא קאכילנא דתנינא: (תהלים קמ"ה) עיני כל
אליך ישברו ואתה נותן להם את אכלם בעתו, בעתם לא נאמר אלא בעתו - מלמד, שכל
אחד ואחד נותן הקב"ה פרנסתו בעתו. אדהכי אתאי אחתיה דרבא דלא חזיא ליה תליסרי
שני, ואתיא ליה תרנגולת פטומה ויין ישן, אמר: מאי דקמא? א"ל: נענתי לך, קום אכול.

Our Rabbis taught: If an orphan applied for assistance to marry, a house must be rented for him, a bed must be prepared for him, and [he is to be supplied with] all [household] objects [needed for] his use, and then he is given a wife in marriage, for it is said in Scripture, "Sufficient for his need in that which he wants" (Devarim 15:8). *"Sufficient for his need," refers to the house; "in that which he wants," refers to a bed and a table; "he" refers to a wife, for so it is said in Scripture, "I will make a fitting helper for him"* (Bereshit 2:18).

Our Rabbis taught: "Sufficient for his need" [implies] you are commanded to maintain him, but you are not commanded to make him rich; "in that which he wants" [includes] even a horse to ride on and a slave to run before him. It was told about Hillel the Elder that for a certain poor man who was of a good family, he bought a horse to ride on and a slave to run before him. On one occasion he could not find a slave to run before him, so he himself [Hillel] ran before him for three miles.

A certain man once applied to R. Nehemiah [for support]. "What do your meals consist of?" [the Rabbi] asked him. "Of fat meat and old wine," the other replied. "Will you consent [the Rabbi asked him] to live with me on lentils?" [The other consented,] lived with him on lentils and died. "Alas," [the Rabbi] said, "for this man whom Nehemiah has killed." On the contrary, he should [have said] "Alas for Nehemiah who killed the man!" [The fact is,] however [that the man himself was to blame, for] he should not have cultivated his luxurious habits to such an extent.

A man once applied to Rava [for support]. "What do your meals consist of?" he asked him. "Of fat chicken and old wine," the other replied. "Did you not consider," the Rabbi asked him, "the burden of the community?" "Do I," the other replied, "eat of theirs? I eat [the food] of the All-Merciful; for we learned, 'the eyes of all wait for You, and You give them their food in due season' (Tehillim 145:15). *Since it is not said 'in* their *season' but 'in* his *season' this teaches that the Hold One, blessed be He, provides for every individual in accordance with his own habits." Meanwhile, Rava's sister, who had not seen him for thirteen years, arrived and brought a fat chicken and old wine. "What a remarkable incident!" [Rava] exclaimed; [then] he said to him, "I apologize to you; come and eat."* **Kebubot 67b**

CONSIDER THIS!

It happened that our Rabbis came to a man called Bar Bohin in connection with a collection of contributions for the maintenance of students. They heard his son say to him, "What are we going to eat today?" He said, "Endives." [The son said,] "of those which you get one measure or two measures for a mina [coin]?" He replied, "Of those which you get two for a mina, for they are withered and cheap." The Rabbis said, "How can we come to such a person first? Let us go on and do out business in the city, and then return to him," After they had done their business in the city, they came to him and said, "Give us a charitable donation." He said, "Go to my wife, and she will give you a measure of denari [coins]." They went to her and said, "Your husband bids you give us a measure of denari." She said to them, "A heaped measure or an exact one?" They said, "He did not specify which." She said, "I will give you a heaped measure, and if my husband says, 'Why?' I will say, 'I gave it to them from my dowry.'" They went to the husband and said, "May your Creator supply your needs." He said to them, "How did she give to you, a heaped measure or an exact one?" They replied, "We did not specify which measure to her, but she said, 'I shall give you a heaped measure, and if my husband asks me why I have given it to you, I will say that I will deduct it from my dowry.'" He said, "It was my wish to give you that way. Why did you not come to me first?" They said to him, "We heard your son asking you, 'What shall we eat today,' and you said, 'Endives,' and he said 'Of those that one gets one measure for a mina or of those which one gets two?' And you said, 'Of those which one gets two, because they are withered and cheap.' We thought: "does a man who has much money to eat endives of which one gets two measures for a mina?'" He replied, "In what concerns myself I can do as I like, but in regard to that which is commanded me by my Creator, I have no power or authority." **Esther Rabbah 11:3**

TZEDAKAH FOR THE 21ST CENTURY

The following section has been excerpted from, *"You Shall Strenghten Them,"*—A Rabbinic Letter on the Poor by Rabbi Elliot N. Dorff, New York: Rabbinical Assembly, April 1999, pp. 30-34.

Some guidelines clearly emerge from Jewish concepts and law regarding the donor, the receiver, or the society in which they live. In light of the fact that God's image is embedded in each of us, we must determine the recipients of aid, the donors, the methods or collection and distribution, the programs of prevention, and all other related factors in this are by asking: What is the most practical and efficient way of caring for the poor while preserving the dignity and economic viability of all concerned?

PREVENTION OF POVERTY

Since the best aid by far is prevention of poverty in the first place, the clear mandate of the Jewish tradition is to support governmental and private programs of education in general and job training in particular. These programs pay multiple dividends, keeping whole groups of the population from a life of unemployment, degradation, and often crime, and enabling them to become productive and dignified members of society. If assistance is necessary, for both practical and moral reasons, it is better to offer employment, a loan, or investment capital to poor people than to give money as a dole. A loan or investment has the potential for making the poor person self-supporting, thus eliminating the drain on the community's resources. It also preserves the dignity of the poor person now and, if the venture succeeds, for the long run.

THE COMMUNITY FEEDS THE HUNGRY

On a communal level, immediate sustenance should be available for the truly destitute with few, if any, questions asked. Programs like Mazon and Sova do this now on an ongoing basis. Similarly, Los Angeles Jewish Aids Services, for example, sponsors a soup kitchen for Jewish AIDS patients and their families ("Project Chicken Soup") and there are undoubtedly other local programs of this sort. Many synagogues and Jewish Family Service agencies collect money for the needy before Passover and Purim. Food may also be provided to the hungry by giving them food stamps or other supermarket vouchers rather than by running a soup-kitchen or food pantry. In addition to these private efforts, government assistance helps millions of people. Jewish law holds us responsible for ensuring that our combined efforts supply food to the hungry in adequate quantities and with sufficient regularity to meet their nutritional needs, just as these needs were met in the soup-kitchens of long ago.

THE COMMUNITY GIVES SHELTER TO THE HOMELESS

Jewish communities made arrangements of varying sorts for the poor. Since the 1980's, severe cutbacks in government support for mental health facilities and for housing programs for the poor have forced thousands of people to live on America's streets. Some synagogues have opened their doors to the homeless on an ongoing basis. These synagogue shelters provide a warm sleeping place and a hot meal about 10-15 homeless men who have begun to find jobs and get back on their feet. Many of the synagogue shelters rely on nightly teams of volunteers who staff the shelter and help the men.

RESPONDING TO BEGGERS ON THE STREET

- Have you ever been approached by someone on the street asking for money?
- Would you give someone money if they asked? What if they appeared inebriated?
- What else could you do for that person?

Jewish law requires that we give something to those who ask—or, if we cannot, that we at least treat them kindly. Jewish law intended, though, that we provide food for the hungry; if the begger is asking for money, and if he or she is clearly inebriated or under the influence of drugs, we need not give this person money to feed his/her habit. On the contrary, that would be "placing a stumbling block before the blind," a violation of Vayikra 19:14. To avoid this problem, some people keep food coupons with them that can be redeemed at various food establishments. No one is obliged by Jewish law to supply people who ask for help under such circumstances with large sums of money. It may, in fact, be counterproductive, for ultimately we do not want to encourage people to beg on the streets; we want them instead to get help from the agencies that we have created to supply assistance with continuity and with the professional expertise to assess and respond to people's actual needs.

When people who are not under the influence of drugs or alcohol approach you on the street, knock on your door, or enter a synagogue asking for money, it is often hard to determine whether they are needy or simply manipulating your sense of compassion and the welfare system. There is no easy guideline for dealing with these situations. If possible, it is often best to refer them (and maybe even offer to take them) to the agencies established to deal with these needs, including governmental and private facilities, the Jewish Free Loan Society, and the Jewish Family Services; that both tests their need to get assistance and provides it in the most appropriate way possible. Most often, though, such a referral is not possible, and then it is probably better to give those asking something, knowing full well that you may be the object of deception, rather than pass by someone who is truly in need.

A Greater Understanding of Love Your Neighbor as Yourself

Treat the poor as you would want to be treated if you were poor

The following story was reprinted with permission from Azriel Eisenberg, *Tzedakah: A Way of Life* (West Orange: Behrman House Inc., 1963) pp. 97 ff.

"The Secret"

Once during a severe depression, Rabbi Isaac (Elchanan) and one of his trustees went out collecting for a man who had lost all his wealth at one stroke. This man was well known and honored in the city, so the rabbi decided to keep his name a secret.

The rabbi and his trustee came to the home of a rich man from whom they expected a large sum. Their host greeted them kindly and made them comfortable. Then he asked the purpose of the rabbi's visit.

"We're here for a contribution," answered Rabbi Isaac.

"For community needs?" asked the host.

"For a certain person who is badly in need," replied the rabbi.

"Who is he?"

Rabbi Isaac shook his head. "We cannot reveal his name. He is a man who has suddenly found himself penniless and hungry. He'd be ashamed to have people know he was accepting charity."

The rich man looked from the rabbi to the trustee. His jaw hardened. "I want to know who it is," he insisted. "In fact – I was going to give you twenty-five rubles when you first mentioned a contribution, but I'll make it fifty rubles if you tell me his name."

"Sorry," the rabbi said firmly, shaking his head again. "We won't give away his name."

"A hundred rubles!" cried the rich man stubbornly. "Surely you're going to refuse an amount like that!"

The trustee started to say something, but Rabbi Isaac cut in sharply: "The name is a secret! Give what you wish, but do not argue with me!"

The rich man took a deep breath, closed his eyes, and said, "Four hundred rubles!"

The trustee could not contain himself any longer. "Rabbi! Rabbi! Tell him! Four hundred rubles, Rabbi! We won't have to make another visit! Make him promise to keep it secret! But tell him, tell him!"

Rabbi Isaac stood up and reached for his coat. "I should not have listened to you even this far," he said to his host. "the honor of a man is greater than all the gold and silver in the world." "He turned to the trustee. "Let us leave. We have many other visits to make."

But at these words the rich man seized the rabbi's arm and begged permission for a private word with him in the next room. When they were alone, the host suddenly broke down into tears.

"The truth is, Rabbi," he sobbed, "I'm bankrupt myself. I'm at the end of my rope. I can't give my own family food and shelter much longer. I wanted to come to you for help, but I couldn't stand the idea of everyone in Kovno hearing about my failure."

"Forgive me, my son," said Rabbi Isaac Elchanan gravely, "for not understanding your trouble. So you tested me to see if I would keep Tzedakah secret or not. Well, now you know. I will collect for you too, my son, and your name will never be mentioned."

The rabbi went back into the other room where the trustee was pacing the floor.

"Well, Rabbi," the trustee asked excitedly, "how much? How much did he give you?"

Rabbi Isaac smiled, "It's a secret," he said.

➢ **How does Rabbi Isaac's action at the end of the story compare with the sources you have studied about how to collect tzedakah?**

In Jewish tradition, the act of gemilut hasadim that is most highly praised is the act of *Halvayat HaMet* (accompanying the dead)–caring for the body from the time of death until it is buried. Most people do not like to think about death, and they are even more uncomfortable thinking about preparing a human body for burial. Nevertheless, it is this preparation and the actual burial itself that Judaism values as the greatest kindness one person can show to another.

Nihum Avelim – comforting mourners – is another act of gemilut hasadim. Throughout the centuries, Jews have helped each other to face the sorrow of bereavement. A number of customs that show sensitivity to the mourners and their needs have developed among the Jewish people.

Some modern Jewish communities are attempting to attend to the mitzvot of *Halvayat HaMet* and *Nihum Avelim* in active, straightforward, respectful, and loving ways. Before you begin this chapter, think about why the name of this mitzvah—Hesed Shel Emet—does not have the words "death" or "burial," in it? Judaism calls the caring of the body from the time of death until it is buried "The Most Truthful Kindness—Hesed Shel Emet"

➢ Why do you think that it is called the "Greatest" or "Most truthful" kindness?

EXERCISE: Decisions and Emotions

When a person dies, his close relatives are faced with two tasks:

1. **Making decisions about care of the body and its burial;**
2. **Facing the reality of the death and their own feelings about it.**

Discuss what some of those decisions and emotions might be, and record them below.

Decisions	Emotions

Jewish texts can serve as a guide to help a person deal with those difficult emotions, and to make some of those hard decisions at such a difficult time. Use the Jewish texts in this chapter to get a sense of what a Jewish response to death is. Think about factors like the role of community, the role of the family, the laws that surround the burial and the mourning period.

Read the following text from Bereshit 47:29 and Rashi's comment that follows it:

וַיִּקְרְבוּ יְמֵי־יִשְׂרָאֵל לָמוּת וַיִּקְרָא ׀ לִבְנוֹ לְיוֹסֵף וַיֹּאמֶר לוֹ אִם־נָא מָצָאתִי חֵן בְּעֵינֶיךָ
שִׂים־נָא יָדְךָ תַּחַת יְרֵכִי וְעָשִׂיתָ עִמָּדִי חֶסֶד וֶאֱמֶת אַל־נָא תִקְבְּרֵנִי בְּמִצְרָיִם׃

And when the time approached for Israel to die, he summoned his son Joseph and said to him, "Do me this favor, place your hand under my thigh as a true act of kindness; please do not bury me in Egypt."
Bereshit 47:29

חסד ואמת. חסד שעושין עם המתים הוא חסד של אמת' שאינו מצפה ו לתשלום גמול:

"A true act of kindness" – kindness that is done for the dead is a true act of kindness since one does it without expecting any repayment. Rashi on Bereshit 47:29

- ➢ Why did Israel (Jacob) ask Joseph to do a 'true act of kindness'?
- ➢ Does Judaism attribute a sense of sanctity to death?
- ➢ Why is burying the dead the highest form of lovingkindness—hesed shel emet?

KAVOD HA MET—HONORING THE DEAD

When hearing of death, one says:

בָּרוּךְ דַּיַּן הָאֱמֶת

"Praised be the righteous Judge."

- ➢ How do you feel saying these words upon hearing about the death of someone you knew?
- ➢ How do you feel saying these words upon hearing about the death of a close relative?
- ➢ Why do we speak of God as a judge at a time of death?
- ➢ When else do we refer to God as a judge? (Think about the daily liturgy in the siddur)

One way of understanding these words is that they acknowledge the fact that there are some things in life over which we as human beings have no control. Death is surely one of those things. For those who might feel guilt or responsibility upon hearing of the death of someone they knew, saying these words is recognition that they personally had nothing to do with causing the death. For those who are less intimately involved, the words are a reminder that people do not control the time of death—and are not in control of many things that are central to the human experience.

FROM THE TIME OF DEATH UNTIL BURIAL: HEVRA KADDISHA

The principal governing the care of the body immediately following death is the sacredness of man. A human being is equated with a Torah scroll that was impaired and can no longer be used at religious services. While the ancient scroll no longer serves any useful ritual purpose, it is revered for the exalted function it once filled. Although the pulse of life is no more, the human form must be respected because of the character and personality it once housed. The manner of respect is governed and detailed by religious tradition rather than by personal sentiment and whim alone. The following are some basic guidelines for the care of the deceased at the time of death:

1. From the moment of death until burial, the deceased may not be left alone. Therefore, the family must arrange for a person called a *shomer* (guard or watcher) to be at his side at all times. The rabbi, funeral director, or Hevra Kaddisha can make such arrangements, but the mourner should ascertain clearly that there will be a *shomer* available. The *shomer* may be a member of the family or a close friend. He remains awake during the entire period of watching. He should read from the Book of Psalms or other appropriate literature.

   In the following selection, the Rabbis of the Talmud wanted to make sure that the person who had died would receive the utmost respect. If there had not been a burial society in place to care for the deceased, the entire town would have been forced to stop working and ensure that a proper burial would take place.

> ואמר רב יהודה אמר רב: מת בעיר - כל בני העיר אסורין בעשיית מלאכה. רב המנונא איקלע לדרומתא, שמע קול שיפורא דשכבא. חזא הנך אינשי דקא עבדי עבידתא, אמר להו: ליהוו הנך אנשי בשמתא לא שכבא איכא במתא? אמרו ליה: חבורתא איכא במתא. - אמר להו: אי הכי - שריא לכו.
>
> *Rav Judah also said this, quoting Rav: "When a person dies in town, all the townspeople are forbidden from doing work." R. Hamnuna once came to Darumata. He heard the sound of the funerary-bugle and seeing some people carrying on their work, he said, "Let the people be under the ban. Is there not a person dead in town?" They told him that there was a Society [to care for the dead] in the town. "If so," he said to them, "you are allowed [to work]."*
> Mo'ed Katan 27b

2. Personal behavior in the room of the deceased should be consonant with the highest degree of respect. There should be no eating, drinking, or smoking; no derogatory remarks about the deceased may be voiced. Discussion in the room should concentrate solely on the deceased and his personal qualities, or on the funeral arrangements.
   Adapted from Maurice Lamm, *The Jewish Way in Death and Mourning*, New York: Jonathan David, 1972

3. Another expression of reverence for the body is washing or purification before burial. Known as *taharah* (purification), this act is usually performed by members of the Hevra Kaddisha, the Burial Society (literally, the "Holy Society"). The body is washed thoroughly from head to foot. Originally the custom was for each cemetery to have a

taharah room for this purpose; today, when almost all funerals take place at funeral parlors, it is done on those premises.

4. One may will his eyes, other organs, or tissue of his body for transplantation into other bodies for healing purposes, because there is no greater *K'vod HaMet* (honor given to the dead) than to bring healing to the living. However, the dead body must be treated respectfully and the remains must be given proper burial.

5. The Jewish way of burial is to place the body into the earth, as suggested in the biblical verse, "and to dust you shall return" (Bereshit 3:19). Hence, there is a traditional ruling against cremation (burning of the dead body).

6. Embalming (treatment of the dead body with drugs or chemicals to prevent decay) is permitted only as a result of specific conditions, such as sanitary reasons, civil law requirements, or the necessary delay or burial. In such cases, embalming is permitted as an act of *K'vod HaMet.* If the embalming process involves the removal of certain parts of the body, those parts should be put into a container and buried together with the body.

7. Tradition objects to dressing the deceased in fine clothing. Hence it prescribes the use of shrouds, handmade cloth of plain linen. This custom became the central symbol of the equality of Jewish burial practice.

8. Similarly, the use of the plainest wooden coffin—generally with wooden pegs rather than metal nails—is recommended, both to maintain the simple equality of all in death, and to follow the principle of "dust you are and dust you shall return."

9. Jewish tradition frowns upon viewing the body. It has become the prevalent secular custom to have the body on exhibition the night before the funeral. This is contrary to Jewish tradition, which prescribes that paying respects should be done at the funeral, and consoling the mourners should begin after the burial, at the home of the mourner. It is also an added burden on the family to be taxed with these social formalities when their hearts are heavy with sorrow, and when they would prefer to be left alone. **Adapted from Isaac Klein,** ***A Time to be Born, a Time to Die, New York: United Synagogue Youth, 1976***

Read and analyze the following Talmud text from Mo'ed Katan.

תנו רבנן: בראשונה היו מוליכין בבית האבל, עשירים - בקלתות של
כסף ושל זהב, ועניים - בסלי נצרים של ערבה קלופה. והיו עניים מתביישים, התקינו
שיהו הכל מביאין בסלי נצרים של ערבה קלופה, מפני כבודן של עניים. תנו רבנן:
בראשונה היו משקין בבית האבל, עשירים - בזכוכית לבנה, ועניים בזכוכית צבועה,
והיו עניים מתביישין. התקינו שיהו הכל משקין בזכוכית צבועה, מפני כבודן של
עניים. בראשונה היו מגלין פני עשירים ומכסין פני עניים, מפני שהיו מושחרין פניהן
מפני בצורת, והיו עניים מתביישין. התקינו שיהו מכסין פני הכל, מפני כבודן של
עניים. בראשונה היו מוציאין עשירים בדרגש, ועניים בכליכה, והיו עניים מתביישין,
התקינו שיהו הכל מוציאין בכליכה, מפני כבודן של עניים.

Our Rabbis taught: Formerly they used to convey [victuals] to the house of mourning, the rich in silver and gold baskets and the poor in baskets of peeled willow twigs, and the poor felt shamed; they therefore instituted that all should convey [victuals] in baskets of peeled willow twigs out of deference to the poor.

Our Rabbis taught: Formerly they used to serve drinks in a house of mourning, the rich in white glass vessels and the poor in colored glass, and the poor felt shamed; they instituted therefore that all should serve drinks in colored glass, out of deference to the poor. Formerly they used to uncover the face of the rich and cover the face of the poor, because their faces turned livid in years of drought and the poor felt shamed; they therefore instituted that everybody's face should be covered, out of deference to the poor. Formerly they used to bring out the rich [for burial] on an ornamented bed and the poor on a plain bier, and the poor felt shamed; they instituted therefore that all should be brought out on a plain bier, out of deference for the poor. Mo'ed Katan 27a-b

Can you differentiate between the actions discussed in the text that give dignity to the living and those that show honor for the dead?

- Mo'ed Katan defines a principle that dictates much of Jewish practice in caring for the deceased until the time of burial and in comforting the mourners. What is the principle?
- Does this text show that the Rabbis wanted to honor the dead?
- Why did the decisions of the Rabbis in this text always favor the sensitivities of the poor?
- What do you think they were trying to say about the nature of death—and to some extent—about the nature of life?

THE FUNERAL

It is accepted Jewish practice for the funeral to take place within 24 hours after the moment of death. Some exceptions include delaying the funeral in order for close relatives to arrive (their presence gives honor to the dead) or transporting the body to Israel for burial there. Expediting the funeral helps mourners to deal with the trauma of the death of a loved one. Historically, it was considered disrespectful to leave the dead unburied for any length of time.

The service at the funeral home includes the recitation of Psalms and the prayer *Ayl Maley Rahamim,* "Lord who is full of mercy." At this time eulogies – speeches that recall and praise the deeds of the dead—are given. In order to show respect, friends carry the coffin from the funeral home to the hearse, and upon arrival at the cemetery, from the hearse to the grave. This act is another example of Hesed Shel Emet, an act of true lovingkindness, which is selfless and can never be repaid.

THE BURIAL

As the coffin is placed in the grave, the words, "May he/she come to his/her place in peace." Are recited. The mourners and friends cover the coffin with spadefuls of dirt. Hearing the dirt fall on the coffin is an important step toward the mourner's accepting the finality of death. Before leaving the gravesite, those attending the funeral should completely cover the coffin with earth; some people prefer to remain until the entire grave is filled.

A TIME FOR REFLECTION

- What do you think the purpose of a Hevra Kaddisha is?
- Do you have a Hevra Kaddisha in your community?
- What is the relationship of the community to the Hevra Kaddisha?
- How does being a member of a Hevra Kaddisha enphasize that the mitzvah of helping to bury the dead is the greatest kindness?
- Do you think it is an honor to be a member of the Hevra Kaddisha? How would you feel about being a member of a Hevra Kaddisha?
- How does a Hevra Kaddisha function in modern times—and what would the differences be (if any) from the work of the Hevra Kaddisha in the past?

Jewish Law is very specific about the requirements for burial and the proper care of the body.

- What kinds of abuses do you think might occur if there is not Hevra Kaddisha?
- Why do you think they might occur?
- How might a Hevrah Kaddisha prevent them?

EXERCISE: Examining the Rituals

List some of the ways that Judaism gives honor to the dead—Kavod HaMet—prior to burial.

1.____

____

2.____

____

3.____

____

4.____

____

5.____

____

6.____

____

AFTER THE BURIAL: GIVING COMFORT TO THE MOURNERS

From the will of Rabbi Eliezer the Great, who lived during the 11th century:

> *My son! Comfort the mourners, and speak to their heart. The companions of Job were held punishable merely because they reproached when they should have consoled him. Thus it is written, "Ye have not spoken of Me the thing that is right, as My servant Job hath."*

Jewish tradition involves the whole Jewish community in helping a mourner overcome the shock and sorrow of bereavement. When we help the mourner, we bring out what is best and most human in us.

The Hevra Kaddisha traditionally took over when death was imminent and relieved the family of the many preparations that were to be made at the time of death. This group was an important part of every Jewish community. Membership in the Hevra Kaddisha was an honor bestowed only upon the pious of the community.

Although rabbis, family counselors, and funeral directors give professional help to bereaved families, the average community member can provide the mourners with a kind of support that is most important. Judaism has imposed some mitzvot upon each individual in order to help the bereaved over this difficult experience.

Performing the mitzvah of *Nihum Avelim,* "consoling the mourners," begins immediately after burial, while the mourners are still at the cemetery. Those present, displaying emotional support with a physical symbol, form two lines through which the mourners walk.

When the mourners return home, however, and the absence of their dear one is stark and tangible, *Nihum Avelim* begins to function in full force.

The first meal that mourners eat should be prepared and served by friends and neighbors. This meal is called *Seudat Havra'ah* –the meal of consolation. The practical reason for this arrangement is that the mourners are not likely to think of preparing food or of eating. Another reason is that the meal and community support serve as a source of comfort and consolation. The mourners usually suffer from a sense of guilt, a feeling of loneliness, or of being forsaken by man and God. Having friends provide and serve the first meal shows the mourners in a very concrete way that other people do care about them.

At the *Se'udat Havra'ah,* the foods served have a symbolic meaning, and enhance the aspect of comfort and consolation to the mourners. They lessen the feeling of guilt by reminding the mourner that death is the fate of all people. The meal usually contains foods that are round, such as eggs, lentils, chickpeas, etc.—symbolizing the wheel of fate that spares no one as it turns. Eggs have an additional meaning; they are a symbol of new life, hope and regeneration.

Visiting the mourners when they observe Shiva (the first week after death) is also part of 'consoling mourners.' It is a sacred obligation incumbent upon every Jew to comfort the mourners, whether a relative, a close friend, or just a mere acquaintance.

The visit can take the form of helping with the chores in the Shiva house (something the mourner in his present condition finds difficult), joining in the religious services that are usually conducted in a house of mourning, or just sitting in silence showing by one's mere presence that he shares the sorrow of the mourner. Leave it to the mourner to speak first.

אמר רבי יוחנן: אין מנחמין רשאין לומר דבר עד שיפתח אבל.

Rabbi Yohanan said, "Comforters are not permitted to say a word until the mourner begins the conversations." Mo'ed Katan 28b

- Did you ever feel obligated to speak when visiting a mourner? Why?

- Why do you think Jewish tradition insists on specific mourning practices and behaviors in comforting mourners?

- Wouldn't it be best simply to allow every mourner and comforting visitor to do what they want to do naturally?

It is a misconception that it is best to distract the mourner so that he forgets his bereavement. On the contrary, it is altogether proper to speak about the deceased, his qualities, hopes and concern for his loved ones. People often feel that such talk will renew the anguish brought by death, and will recall the pain and agony of the deceased. Far from doing that, it gives the bereaved a chance to reminisce and to express his grief aloud. This is of great therapeutic value.

The occasion should be a means of expressing sympathy to the mourners, not of indulging in small talk that sometimes borders on the vulgar. It should not be turned into a social event. This is a good opportunity to study suitable sacred texts.

If people wish to bring gifts, they may do so, but care should be taken that the gift fits the occasion. The most appropriate give prevalent today is a contribution to the deceased's favorite charity or to the synagogue where she or she worshipped.

WELCOMING MOURNERS IN THE SYNAGOGUE

Another occasion for offering condolences is at Friday night services. It is customary in many synagogues that on the first Shabbat at services after the funeral, the mourner waits in the lobby outside the sanctuary during Lecha Dodi. Just before they begin Psalm 92, which officially ushers in the Sabbath. The mourners are then invited to enter, and the worshippers greet them with the traditional words of condolence:

הַמָּקוֹם יְנַחֵם אֶתְכֶם בְּתוֹךְ שְׁאָר אֲבֵלֵי צִיּוֹן וִירוּשָׁלָיִם

"May the Lord comfort you among the other mourners for Zion and Jerusalem."

- Why do you think that mourners wait outside until after the Lecha Dodi?
- How does this sentence give comfort to mourners?
- How do you feel when you say it?
- How would you feel to hear someone else say it to you?
- What do you notice about the words of condolence that the mourner is greeted with vis a vis community?

EXERCISE

Create another verse to be said when a mourner returns to the synagogue?

___

___

___

SHIVA—COMMUNITY'S RESPONSIBILITY TO THE MOURNER

It is an early weekday morn. A quiet residential street of the dynamic city is still enveloped in a drowsy stillness. Soon life will awake in its silent comfortable houses and noisy children, after a hasty breakfast, will leap through doors, school-ward bound. Men can be seen entering one of the houses. Their bearing is marked by reverence and solemnity. Sorrow has recently visited one of the homes on the street and friends are gathering for the mourning service. Within the residence, candles are lit, tefillin and talesim are quietly donned and the voice of prayer is heard in the hushed atmosphere.

Long ago a people developed this practice so rich in meaning that neither the passing of centuries nor the roaring life of a metropolitan center has been able to render it obsolete. The friends are no longer individuals come to express sympathy, each in his particular way, with the feeling that the degree of his own friendship with the mourners dictates. The individuals have merged into a "minyan" a congregation. They have coalesced into an "eidah," a community. Though this community is small in numbers, it represents in every religious detail the larger K'lal Yisroel of which each identified Jew is part. Thus does a community symbolically and actually share in the sorrow of one of its members. The grief of the individual re-echoes in the life of the group. No Jew stands alone in his bereavement, while his personal anguish serves as a wall between him and all those upon whose way in life the dark shadow has not fallen. A people closes ranks and encircles it stricken member with the warmth of brotherly sympathy.

The religious service of this little group, representing the larger community, takes place in the home. It is a tribute to the central position of the home. Where a family lives and loves and fashions the most intimate bonds to link persons one to the other – you have a sanctuary appropriate for worship. For the home is a sanctuary no less than the Synagogue. Its holiness is of no lesser kind than that which the formal house of prayer of the entire community is invested. The poignancy and sanctity of grief are best expressed in the intimate sanctuary of the home. The sanctuary of the home can never be replaced by Synagogue or Temple, however large or magnificent.

The prayer is concluded. The imperatives of modern living compel the minyan to dissolve once again into its component individuals who hurry through streets, now filled with romping and laughing children and speeding automobiles, to offices, shops and plants. The mourners remain. They are, however, no longer completely alone. In the atmosphere of their home the prayers linger and bespeak the solace of a tradition and the brotherhood of a community.

Reprinted from Morris Adler, "We Do Not Stand Alone," in *A Treasury of Comfort*, ed. By Sidney Greenberg (New York: Crown Publishers, Inc., 1954) pp. 133-4.

EXERCISE: Community Actions

List the different acts of personal service the community performs for the mourners during Shiva:

1.____

____

2.____

____

3.____

____

4.____

____

5.____

____

6.____

____

Put an asterisk (*) next to those you have performed. Circle those you would like to do when the need arises.

- ➢ What does the Jewish community do at the time of death?
- ➢ What makes the Jewish response to death so unique?
- ➢ How do the members of one's extended family – a smaller community – react at the time of a death? What actions do you think they believe to be their specific responsibilities?

The Mitzvah of Hesed Shel Emet can never be repaid by the person you are doing it for. That is truly the reason it is called, The Great Kindness.

Guide to the Hevrah Kadisha

Adopted by the Committee on Congregational Standards of the United Synagogue of Conservative Judaism
October 27, 1965
Reviewed June 1998

Preamble: the Guide to the Hevrah Kadisha is to be regarded as complementary to the Guide to Funeral Practices of the United Synagogue. The Hevrah Kaddisha is the name given to the congregational committee or organization whose purpose it is to perform the mitzvah of preparing the deceased for burial in accordance with the Jewish tradition. The following suggestions are presented to all our congregations in the hope that they may prove helpful to those Hevrut Kadisha now functioning as well as to new ones which may be formed.

COMPOSITION OF THE HEVRAH KADISHA

1. The Hevrah Kadisha shall be a standing committee of the congregation functioning under the guidance of and with the cooperation of the Rabbi and Hazan. In some congregations, the Hevrah Kadisha is a separate corporation though legally associated with the congregation.

2. Congregations may find it advisable to join with other congregations in forming a common Hevrah Kadisha to serve all associate for this purpose.

3. The Hevrah Kadisha should be a committee distinct and apart from the Cemetery Committee. Where such separation is not feasible, the committees may be merged.

4. The duties of the Hevrah Kadisha are among the most important mitzvot incumbent upon us. Membership should be regarded as a distinct honor carrying with it the appreciation and respect of the entire congregation. Members of the Hevrah Kadisha include men and women who serve and perform their duties willingly and piously.

In some congregations, members of the Hevrah Kadisha are honored annually by a special congregational dinner, usually on the seventh day of the Hebrew month of Adar, the Yahrzeit of Moses and the traditional day for the annual meeting and Seudat Mitzvah of the Hevrah Kadisha.

THE DUTIES OF THE HEVRAH KADISHA

A. INITIAL ARRANGEMENTS

1. In the areas where there are Jewish funeral establishments, the Hevrah Kadisha stands in readiness to arrange for the funeral of the deceased, the date and the hour, in consultation with the bereaved family, the Rabbi and the Hazan.

2. In areas where there are no Jewish funeral establishments, the Hevrah Kadisha shall, with permission, relieve the family of this task and together with the Rabbi and Hazan make the arrangements itself.

B. TAHARAH

1. The Hevrah Kadisha shall arrange for the Taharah, the ritual washing of the body. The Taharah rite should preferably be performed by members of the Hevrah Kadisha. This is the practice in most Hevrot Kadisha. Where this is not possible, persons hired especially for this purpose may be used.

2. Tachrichim (white linen shrouds) shall be used to clothe the deceased. Other garments shall not be used. This is in keeping with the Jewish tradition that in death all are equal.

3. Every adult male shall, in addition to the tachrichim, be buried with a kipah and a talit which has been rendered pasul, namely in a talit from which one fringe has been removed.

C. SHOMRIM

1. A Jewish tradition requires that the deceased be attended to continuously from the moment of death until burial and that his/her memory be honored by the reading of Psalms during the night before the funeral by shomrim (watchers).

D. FUNERAL

1. Interment traditionally occurs no later than one day after death. Under exceptional circumstances, the Rabbi should be consulted.

2. To emphasize the equality of all of death, Jewish tradition calls for simplicity and bars ostentatious display. The Guide to Funeral Practices of the United Synagogue should be consulted and followed.

3. The Hevrah Kadisha shall offer assistance in arranging for a burial plot in conjunction with the Cemetery Committee.

E. PERIOD OF MOURNING

1. During the Shivah period, the Hevrah Kadisha or other appropriate committee shall assure wherever possible that a minyan convenes morning and evening at the home of the mourner.

2. It should provide prayer books, talitot, kipot and tefillin.

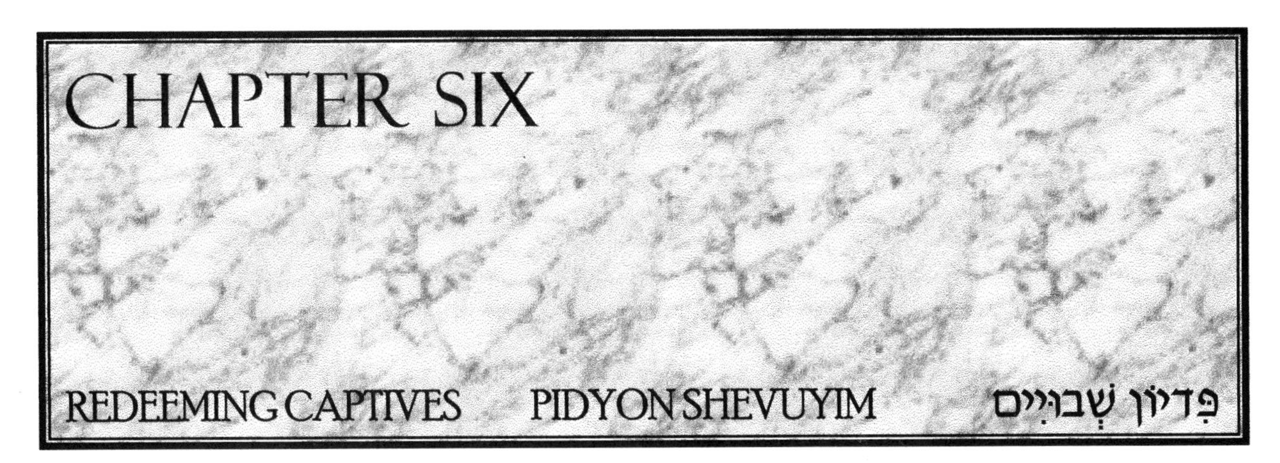

FOCUS ON: JUDITH FELD CARR—MITZVAH HERO

In 1972, after hearing about the devastating oppression under which the Jews in Syria were living, Judy Feld Carr, of Toronto, began a secret relief operation that would last more than 23 years. She started out by sending care packages containing religious objects to Syria, under the condition that no one knew the source. When her husband, and partner in this project died only a year after this project began, she continued to use her late husbands name in order to keep a low profile. After her husband's untimely death, her congregation, Beth Tzedec created the Dr. Ronald Feld Fund for Jews in Arab Lands. Contributions to this fund helped Feld Carr continue her work. After six years of sending packages to Jews in Syria, Feld Carr decided to add rescue to her relief missions, and by 1978, Syrian Jews were being smuggled out of Syria. For 23 years, Feld Carr used any resources she could, including bribing judges and local officials in order to help the Syrian Jews leave their oppressive land.

To say that Judy Feld Carr is a hero is an understatement. Over the course of 23 years, she saved the lives of more than 2500 Syrian Jews living under oppression. She has been recognized by the State of Israel for her heroic efforts, and personally by the late Prime Minister of Israel, Yitzchak Rabin who said:

"Words cannot express my gratitude to you for 23 years of hard and dangerous work, during which you devoted your time and your life to the Jewish community in Syria. The Jews of Syria who were rescued and the State of Israel owe you so much, and will never be able to reward you as you deserve."

INTRODUCTION

Pidyon Shevuyim is the mitzvah of redeeming captives. From the earliest centuries of our history as a nation, we have been faced with the necessity of gaining our freedom. During many historical periods, large numbers of our people were enslaved or held captive; during others, individuals were the objects of kidnapping and imprisonment for the sake of ransom. We are well aware of the problem of soldiers missing in action. During and after the Vietnam War, Jews and non-Jews alike have felt pain and sorrow for the POW's/MIA's and their families. Frequently we were able to buy our freedom and the freedom of our brothers. Sometimes, however, even money has been insufficient to redeem Jews held captive, and other means have been sought to secure their freedom.

➢ How can we agree on a modern definition of the word 'captive' in modern terms?

➢ What are some situations in modern Jewish history when Jews were held captive or hostage?

Think about this: Being a captive means being dependent upon the will of some power greater than the Jewish community. Captivity may also be defined by the desire of the captor to exact some payment, penalty or recognition from those who wish to save the captive. When a Jewish Community has limited funds and cannot ransom all the captives that need redeeming, there would understandably be a great deal of time that might be wasted deciding the issue. Jewish Law tries to save this valuable time by setting priorities to assure that at least someone will be saved from captivity.

FREEDOM

Many celebrations in Judaism focus on the importance of our freedom. When we pray, we are reminded that being free is a tremendously important concept in Jewish life. Nevertheless, even today, many people—Jews and non-Jews alike—are not free to choose how or where they live, and how they express their religious values and practices. Over the past fifty years, The Jewish community world wide, led by the State of Israel, has rallied in large numbers in support of the release of Jews from the Former Soviet Union, Ethiopia, and Syria.

➢ What do you know about the stories of the Jews from the three mentioned places?

➢ Have you ever participated in a project that involved raising awareness for the release of Jews from these communities? (e.g. rallies for Soviet Jewry, Israel's MIA's, letter writing, etc.)

The Jewish community has traditionally felt the need to help other Jews who were captives. Jews felt this need for a number of reasons: they believed that every Jews was responsible for other Jews. They recognized the possibility that they too might someday be captives of some regime or another—and would want their brothers to work on their behalf for their freedom. They believed that captivity ultimately would result in the loss of the lives of the captives—and Jews were willing to make great sacrifices in order to save lives—Jewish or non-Jewish.

כָּל יִשְׂרָאֵל עֲרֵבִים זֶה בָּזֶה

All Israel is Responsible for One Another

➢ Why do you think that the Jewish community worldwide has a responsibility to help other Jewish communities around the world?

➢ How do you think that the Jewish community has a responsibility to help communities in need around the world that are not Jewish?

We live in countries where many of us take our freedom for granted. In our Jewish communities, we never have to hide our shabbat candles, sneak into our synagogues or sell prayer books, kippot or t'fillin underground. Our government does not suppress our voice as a community. In fact, throughout the United States and Canada, the Jewish community is one of the most powerful voices on the political scene today.

Israel and the North American Jewish community have worked together to free massive amounts of oppressed Jews from communities in Europe, the Former Soviet Union, Ethiopia and Syria. Many of the largely populated oppressed Jewish communities around the world have already been freed and are now living in Israel and throughout the Diaspora.

THESE ARE THEIR STORIES...

Operation Magic Carpet

On the day that Israel was created in 1948, its Jewish inhabitants numbered a little over 600,000. Within three years, that population had almost doubled, in what was perhaps the quickest demographic growth of any nation in history. The explosion in numbers was due to two enormous migrations: Holocaust survivors and Jews from the Arab world.

When World War II ended, many Jewish survivors of Hitler found themselves shifted from "concentration camps" to DP (Displaced Persons) camps. Those survivors who wanted to go to Palestine quickly learned that the British allowed very few Jews in. Jews caught fleeing to Palestine were sent back to Europe or to British DP camps on the nearby Island of Cyprus. Shortly after Israeli statehood was declared, fifty-two refugee camps were closed in Europe, as were the Cypriot DP camps: Within a few years, more than 200,000 Holocaust survivors were brought to Israel.

At the same time, the creation of Israel accelerated the deterioration of Jewish life in the Arab world. Arab Jews fearing for their lives, fled Egypt, Iraq, Syria and Yemen en masse, leaving behind small remnants of formerly large communities. In almost every instance, Arab governments confiscated the property of the fleeing Jews, many of whom were rich. As a result, most arrived in Israel penniless. Israel itself was a very poor country in 1948, and little money was available to help integrate the new immigrants. Many, but not exclusively, Arab Jews were housed in hastily created transit camps. To this day, the recollection of the primitive transit camps arouses deep feelings among the Jews from the Arab world.

One of the more integrated Arab-Jewish communities in Israel came from Yemen. Yemenite Jewry had lived for many centuries in one of the poorest countries in the Arab world. In addition, the anti-Semitic restrictions imposed on them had been in strict accord with fundamentalist Islamic teachings. They were forbidden to wear bright garments, to bear weapons, or to use saddles. They were also compelled to clean the sewers of San'a, Yemen's capital city. Arab school children routinely threw stones at Jews, and when the leaders of the Jewish community tried to have this frightening and dangerous activity outlawed, Muslim religious leaders insisted that it was a religiously mandated custom that could not be forbidden. Yemen itself was so primitive that few inhabitants had even seen an appliance, tool or vehicle operated by electricity. When airplanes started arriving in Yemen to take the Jews to Israel, the deeply pious Jews were reminded of the verse in the Torah, "You have seen...how I bore you on the eagle's wings and brought you to Me." (Exodus 19:4). The rescue became known as "Operation Magic Carpet."

Adapted from Jewish Literacy by Joseph Telushkin, New York: William Morrow & Co., 1991, p. 300-301

Syrian Jewry Relief Efforts

The Jewish presence in Syria dates back to Biblical times and is intertwined with the history of Jews in neighboring Eretz Israel. With the advent of Christianity, restrictions were imposed on the community. The Arab conquest in 636 c.e., however, greatly improved the lot of the Jews. Unrest in neighboring Iraq in the 10th century resulted in Jewish migration to Syria and brought about a boom in commerce, banking, and crafts. During the reign of the Fatimids, the Jew Menashe Ibrahim El-Kazzaz ran the Syrian administration, and he granted Jews positions in the government.

Syrian Jewry supported the aspirations of the Arab nationalists and Zionism, and Syrian Jews believed that the two parties could be reconciled and that the conflict in Palestine could be resolved. However, following Syrian independence from France in 1946, attacks against Jews and their property increased, culminating in the pogroms of 1947, which left all shops and synagogues in Aleppo in ruins. Thousands of Jews fled the country, and their homes and property were taken over by the local Muslims.

For the next decades, Syrian Jews were, in effect, hostages of a hostile regime. They could leave Syria only on the condition that they leave members of their family behind. Thus the community lived under siege, constantly under fearful surveillance of the secret police. This much was allowed due to an international effort to secure the human rights of the Jews, the changing world order, and the Syrian need for Western support; so the conditions of the Jews improved somewhat.

Prior to the initiation of the peace process in the Middle East, the Syrian Jewish community was deprived of many basic human and civil rights. Those who attempted to flee across the borders illegally were usually caught, arrested, and cruelly tortured in the dungeons of the secret police. The plight of Syrian Jewry became an international human rights issue in the mid-1970s. The United States, Canada, and France played leading roles in the efforts to bring justice to the community. The Madrid Conference in 1992 was the turning point for the Jewish community. American and Israeli pressure succeeded in convincing the Syrian government to declare that Jews could leave freely.

Jews of the Former Soviet Union

During the 1970's, over one hundred thousand Soviet Jews decided they did not want to continue living in the Communist Soviet Union. They had been allowed to apply for permission to leave the USSR but must present evidence of close relatives living in Western countries or have invitations from the State of Israel to settle in the Jewish homeland. Laws in the USSR made it difficult for Soviet citizens to obtain exit visas to leave the country. When they did succeed in obtaining the necessary documents, they had to present large sums of money in order to pay exit taxes and to purchase tickets for the long train ride to Vienna. Frequently, the Israeli government subsidized such expenses if Soviet Jews could not afford to pay them. At the border, they could exchange only 100 rubles into foreign currency. In Vienna, they were given the choice of going to Israel (with the aid of the Jewish Agency) or to the

United States, Canada, or other Western countries (with the aid of organizations such as HIAS).

- Vladimir and Carmella lived in Vilnius with their infant son, Moshe. Vladimair was trained to be a molecular biolist; Carmella, to be concert vionist. They applied to leave the Soviet Union and Vladmir lost his job. Fortunately, refuseniks in Vilnius were allowed to work and Vladimir was given a job at the local telephone company. Carmella stayed home but began to paint a Jewish collection, which she would send out of the country with émigrés. She was eager to have her work displayed in Israel and North America where it might help in gathering popular support for the problems of Soviet Jews.

Frequently, Soviet Jews became "Refuseniks," those whom the government refused to permit to leave the Soviet Union. A refusenik generally lost his job, as did members of his immediate family and his parents (whether or not they wanted to emigrate). If he had no official employment, he may have been charged with the crime of "parasitism"—living off the state as a parasite. This was most often punishable by years of imprisonment or internal exile in Siberia.

- Yosif was sentenced to three years of internal exile to Siberia. His crime was basically that he wanted to emigrate to Israel. Yosef had lived in Moscow and applied for an exit visa. He lost his job and was arrested for parasitism. He was sentenced to two years of exile and when he returned, he lost his permit to live in Moscow, which would leave his wife and son alone. Soviet Law at the time mandated that a man must live with his wife—the problem was that he was not allowed to live in Moscow. When he continued to live with his wife in Moscow, he was arrested, tried for passport violations (not having a permit to live in Moscow) and returned to Siberia.

Simultaneous with public protests and marches, the Soviet Jewry groups lobbied actively in Washington. Their most prominent legislative victory was the congressionally sponsored Jackson-Vanik amendment, which linked trade with Russia to freedom of emigration for Soviet Jews. The various Soviet Jewry organizations also encouraged tens of thousands of American and Western Jews to visit Russia as tourists and to spend time with Jewish dissidents. USY sent several groups and individuals to visit Soviet Jews from the late 1960's until the situation changed by the late 1980's.

By the late 1980s, the Soviet-Jewish protest movement had achieved far more than its founders had expected. The large majority of Soviet Jews applying to emigrate were being permitted to do so, and inside the Soviet Union, for the first time since the Communist revolution of 1917, a yeshiva was established. Nonetheless, the moves toward greater democratization introduced inside Russia by President Mikhail Gorbachev also guaranteed greater freedom for anti-Semitic groups. When groups such as the far right wing, ultra nationalist Pamyat started publicly propagating anti-Semitism, beginning around 1988, hundreds of thousands of Jews started clamoring to leave Russia. By early 1990, more than ten thousand were leaving Russia monthly.

Between 1990 and 1996, more than 600,000 Jews left the Former Soviet Union for Israel. That is the same number of people that lived in Israel during the first year of existence in 1948. By the turn of the century, these former Soviet Jews constitute 10% of Israel's population, and the number continues to grow. Many Soviet Jews integrated into Israeli society as doctors, engineers and scientists.

Ethiopian Jews—Israel Makes History Redeeming 14,400 in a 24-hour Airlift

In the Early 1980's, many Ethiopian Jews began leaving their villages in the rural areas and making their way to the southern Sudan, from where they hoped to make their was to Kenya—and from there to Israel. The second stage of their journey from made form the Sudan aboard Israeli Navy craft, which awaited them in the Red Sea and brought them to Israel. The existing Ethiopian Jewish community in Israel numbered around 7,000. By late 1981, 14,000 more Ethiopian Jews had arrived. By mid 1984, this figure doubled.

Mid 1984 saw the beginning of a mass rescue operation, entitled, *"Mivtza Moshe"* [Operation Moses]: over a period of a few months, 8,000 Jews were flown from Khartoum, Sudan to Europe and from there to Israel. News of the rescue leaked out to the foreign media in November 1985, with the result that President Numeiri of Sudan halted the operations for fear of hostile reaction from the Arab states. After mediation by the United States, Numeiri allowed six American Hercules planes to airlift the last remaining Ethiopian Jews in Sudan; their arrival in Israel brought the number of olim to over 16,000.

> FYI:
> *Olim*—from the Hebrew word *Oleh* meaning to ascend, or ascent. Refers to a group of people who made Aliya to live in Israel. Why do you think moving to Israel is called *aliya*—to go up?

In December of 1989, 16 years after the rupture of diplomatic relations between Ethiopia and Israel, the Israeli Embassy in Addis Abbaba was reopened. With the renewal of diplomatic relations, contact was made between people who had left Ethiopia for Israel and those who had remained behind. Families were instructed to make their way to Addis Abbaba and apply to the Embassy to bring them to Israel. By the end of 1990, between 16,000 and 17,000 Ethiopian Jews arrived in Addis Abbaba.

In May of 1991, after Ethiopian dictator Mengistu fled the country, the new regime consented to allow Israel to operate a continuous airlift for a consideration of forty million US dollars. On May 24, 1991, over the holiday of Shavuot, 14,000 people were flown overnight to Israel. This was known as *"Mivtzah Shlomo"* [Operation Solomon], a procedure which took all of 48 hours and during which 7 babies were born. Following this mass rescue, 6,000 more Ethiopian Jews came on aliya.

More than 20,000 Ethiopian Jews came to live in Israel in the early 1990s. Immediately after their arrival, and because of the concurrent timing with the wave of immigration of Jews from the Former Soviet Union, the State of Israel adopted a plan by which housing for these new immigrants would be 85% financed by the government of the State of Israel.
In addition to financial aid, Israel launched special enrichment programs for Ethiopian children. The IDF also became involved in the absorption of the Ethiopian aliya with a range

of special educational programming. By 1999, more than 1500 Ethiopian olim serve in the IDF including 23 officers, and there were a growing number of volunteers applying to combat units.

EXERCISE: AFTER THE ABSORPTION

After reading the amazing stories of these four communities, can you identify some problems that might come about with regard to their absorption into Israeli and/or North American societies? What are some solutions to those problems?

Problem Possible Solution

1. ______________________________

2. ______________________________

3. ______________________________

4. ______________________________

5. ______________________________

EXERCISE: THINKING ABOUT FREEDOMS

As young Jews living in North America, we should be grateful that we will never know what it is like to live under conditions such as what you have read about in this chapter. How can we help to insure that Jews around the world can live their lives freely? List some freedoms that you have that you might take for granted. Think about even the simplest things, such as going to school, attending USY events, etc.

1. ______________________________

2. ______________________________

3. ______________________________

4. ______________________________

PIDYON SHEVUYIM TODAY

While we read about heroic rescue efforts over the last two decades, there are still people around the world who are suffering, and being help captive against their will.

ISRAEL'S MIA's—The Boys Who Never Came Home

Four soldiers—Zachary Baumel, Yehudah Katz and Tzvi Feldman who disappeared after the 1982 battle at Sultan Yaqub in Lebanon and Ron Arad—who was taken prisoner after his jet went down over southern Lebanon in 1986—never came home. Reports indicate that the three soldiers, who were captured by Syrian forces in 1982, were later paraded through the streets of the Syrian capital of Damascus. They were never seen nor heard from again. Zachary Baumel was an American citizen and sergeant in the Israeli Defense Forces. PLO Chairman Yasser Arafat returned half of Baumel's dog tag in 1993, but as late as 1999 there was no further communication.

- What kinds of problems are created for a family when one of its members falls into captivity?
- What are the potential problems and risks to the prisoner? (Physical and psychological abuse, physical and emotional stress, issue of remarriage, issue of not knowing what lies in your future/the future of your loved one)
- How do these factors make you feel about someone who is held hostage?

Free Ron Arad- A Community In Action

Young people have always been among the activists on Jewish communal issues. Enthusiasm for social justice is contagious and their voices and energy have played a vital role in the efforts to return the Israeli MIA's to their families.

On October 16, 1986, Israeli navigator Captain Ron Arad bailed out of his plane on a mission in Lebanon and was captured by members of the Iranian backed Amal terrorist organization. Since then, Ron has been held captive by several such organizations, all of them extremist Shiite groups, all of them backed by Iran. He has been denied basic rights of POW's as set down in the Geneva Convention. The International Red Cross has not been permitted to send or receive letters. While he was in good health when he was captured, nothing is known of his present state of health, or, for that matter anything else about him. Iran claims to know nothing of the matter or of Ron's whereabouts or condition.

While there is some speculation regarding whether or not Ron Arad is still alive in captivity, the Jewish community worldwide continues to rally on his behalf in the hopes that someday he will return home to his wife Tami, and his daughter, Yuval.

EXERCISE: Needs of Captives

List below as many of the needs of captives as you can. (Indicate which needs are related to various kinds of captivity, i.e., Soviet Jews; hijacking victims; Syrian Jews; etc.)

1. ______________________
2. ______________________
3. ______________________
4. ______________________
5. ______________________
6. ______________________
7. ______________________
8. ______________________
9. ______________________
10. ______________________
11. ______________________
12. ______________________

- ➢ Which of these needs could be satisfied by the actions of individuals?
- ➢ Which of these needs could be satisfied by actions of the Jewish community?
- ➢ Which of these needs may not be able to be satisfied at all? Why?

EXERCISE: Placing Priority I

What do you feel should be the order of priority for redeeming the following people listed?

1) Mother	**2) Father**	**3) King of Israel**	**4) Soldier**
5) Teacher	**6) High Priest**	**7) Child**	**8) Scholar**
7) President	**8) Prophet**	**9) Movie Star**	**12) Neighbor**

Highest   Lowest

COMMUNITY RESPONSIBILITY AND PIDYON SHVUYIM

Read the following selection from Horayot 13a. (It might help if you to read them aloud.) Consider the relationships described between a person and their father, mother, teacher, scholar, King of Israel, High Priest, and prophet. Use the biblical references to help you explain the reasoning and priorities of the Rabbis.

מתני׳: האיש קודם לאשה - להחיות ולהשב אבדה, והאשה קודמת לאיש - לכסות ולהוציא מבית השבי. בזמן ששניהם עומדים בקלקלה - האיש קודם לאשה. גמ׳: ת״ר: היה הוא ואביו ורבו בשבי - הוא קודם לרבו, ורבו קודם לאביו, אמו קודמת לכולם. חכם קודם למלך, ישראל חכם שמת - אין לנו כיוצא בו, מלך ישראל שמת - כל ישראל ראוים למלכות. מלך קודם לכהן גדול, שנאמר: (מלכים א׳ א) ויאמר המלך (אליהם) [להם] קחו עמכם (או מעבדי) [את עבדי] אדוניכם וגו׳. כהן גדול קודם לנביא, שנאמר: (מלכים א׳ א) ומשח אותו שם צדוק הכהן ונתן הנביא, הקדים צדוק לנתן; ואומר: (זכריה ג) שמע נא יהושע הכהן הגדול אתה ורעיך וגו׳.

MISHNAH: *A man takes precedence over a woman in matters of life and restoration of lost property and a woman takes precedence over a man in respect of clothing and ransom from captivity. When both are exposed to moral degradation in their captivity, the man's ransom takes precedence over that of the woman.*

GEMARA: *Our Rabbis taught: If a man and his father and his teacher were in captivity he takes precedence over his teacher and his teacher takes precedence over his father, while his mother takes precedence over all of them.*

A scholar takes precedence over a king of Israel, for it a scholar dies there is none to replace him while if a king of Israel dies, all Israel are eligible for kingship.

A king takes precedence over a High Priest, for it is said, "And the king said unto them, 'Take with you the servants of your lord...'" (I Melachim I:33)

A High Priest takes precedence over a prophet, for it is said, "And let Zadok the priest and Nathan the prophet anoint him there..." (I Melachim I:34), *Zadok being mentioned before Nathan. And furthermore it is stated, "Hear now, O Joshua the High Priest, thou and fellows..."* (Zechariah 3:8).
Horayot 13a

EXERCISE: PLACING PRIORITY II

List the order of priority for redeeming captives on the chart below, as taught by Horayot 13a.

Highest — Lowest

Read the following text:

ההוא גברא דהוה מפקיד גביה ארנקא דפדיון שבויים, סליקו גנבי
עילויה, שקלה יהבה ניהלייהו. אתא לקמיה דרבא. פטריה. א"ל אביי: והא מציל
עצמו בממון חבירו הוא. א"ל: אין לך פדיון שבויים גדול מזה.

A certain man had a purse of money deposited with him for the redemption of captives. Being attacked by thieves he took it and handed it over to them. He was thereupon summoned before Rava who nevertheless declared him exempt [from punishment]. Abaye said to him: "Was not that man rescuing himself by means of another man's money?" He replied: "There could hardly be a case of redeeming captives more pressing than this." Bava Kamma 117b

- ➢ What is the special circumstance described in the text?
- ➢ Does it teach something new or does it agree with the teachings of the previous text – Horayot 13?

MAIMONIDES SPEAKS OUT

➢ What should and should not be done in order to save captives?

We learned in Chapter 4—K'vod He'Ani—that poor relatives should be taken care of first and then the poor of one's own immediate vicinity, and then the poor of the city, and then the poor of another city. How can Maimonides—in the very next chapter of the Mishneh Torah, Laws of Gifts to the Poor—say that captives anywhere take precedence over these poor people?

פדיון שבויים קודם לפרנסת עניים ולכסותן, ואין לך מצוה
גדולה כפדיון שבויים שהשבוי הרי הוא בכלל הרעבים והצמאים והערומים ועומד
בסכנת נפשות, והמעלים עיניו מפדיונו הרי זה עובר על לא תאמץ את לבבך ולא
תקפוץ את ידך ועל לא תעמוד על דם רעך ועל לא ירדנו בפרך לעיניך, ובטל מצות
פתח תפתח את ידך לו, ומצות וחי אחיך עמך, ואהבת לרעך כמוך, והצל לקוחים
למות והרבה...

Pidyon Shevuyim takes precedence over supporting the poor or clothing them. There is no greater mitzvah than Pidyon Shevuyim, for the problems of the captive include the problems of the hungry, the thirsty, the naked, and he who is in mortal danger. He who ignores the need to redeem captives transgresses the following (commandments):

1. *Do not harden your heart or shut your hand against your needy kinsman. (Devarim 15:7)*
2. *Do not stand idly by the blood of your neighbor. (Vayikra 19:16)*
3. *He shall not rule ruthlessly over him in your sight. (Vayikra 25:53)*
4. *You shall surely open your hand to him. (Devarim 15:8)*
5. *Love your neighbor as yourself. (Vayikra 19:18)*
6. *Rescue those who are drawn to death. (Mishlei 24:11)*

Mishneh Torah, Laws of Gifts to the Poor, 8:10

EXERCISE: List the Order in Which Captives are to be Redeemed:

After reading these texts, on the provided chart, list Maimonides' order for redeeming captives, and compare it to the order from Horayot 13a.

According to Maimonides	According to Horayot 13a
Highest	Highest
Lowest	Lowest

EXERCISE: WHAT WOULD YOU DO....

Think about how you would answer the following questions and then read the next section to find out what Maimonides said.

1) Inhabitants of a town who have raised funds to build a synagogue but see that performing another mitzvah required the money they have collected. Should they donate the money towards that mitzvah or keep the money for what it was allocated?

2) How much can you collect in ransom for a captive? Can you help them escape?

Consider the following situations in light of the above question:

- In 1976, terrorists hijacked a plane to Entebbe, Uganda and held all Jews (many Israelis) as captives. The Israelis made a basically successful rescue: however, one rescuer, Lt. Colonel Yonaton Netanyahu and three passengers were killed: Jean-Jacques Maimon, Ida Borowicz, and Pasco Cohen. Most people would probably agree that the Israelis did the right thing, even though 4 people died in the process. Do you agree?

- In the Spring of 1980, an American attempt to rescue its hostages in Iran failed before it every really got off the ground. A number of American servicemen were killed, and the Iranian captors separated the hostages from each other making life much harder on the hostages. Was this rescue worth attempting even though lives were lost?

- In 1985, Israel released 1,150 Palestinian and other terrorists—including mass murders—in exchange for three Israeli soldiers who fell into terrorist hands in Lebanon in 1982. Do think this was a fair exchange?

3) If two people—a man and a woman—are in captivity, and both are forced into a situation that might cause them to sin, who takes precedence?

4) If there are many poor people or many captives, but not enough money to support, clothe, or redeem them all, who takes precedence—a Kohen, Levi or Yisrael?

5) If there are two captives—a teacher or your father and a scholar with great wisdom—which takes precedence?

MAIMONIDES' ANSWERS TO "WHAT WOULD YOU DO..."

❶

אנשי העיר שגבו מעות לבנין בית הכנסת ובא להן דבר מצוה מוציאין בו המעות, קנו אבנים וקורות לא ימכרום לדבר מצוה אלא לפדיון שבויים, אע"פ שהביאו את האבנים וגדרום ואת הקורות ופסלום והתקינו הכל לבנין מוכרין הכל לפדיון שבויים בלבד, אבל אם בנו וגמרו לא ימכרו את בית הכנסת אלא יגבו לפדיונן מן הצבור.

Inhabitants of a town who have raised funds to build a synagogue but who see that performing another mitzvah required the money they have collected, should donate the money towards that mitzvah. If they purchased stones and beams (for building the synagogue) they should not sell them in order to perform another mitzvah except Pidyon Shevuyim. Even if they have brought the stones (to the building site) and laid their foundation, and if they have carved the beams, and prepared everything for the building, they may sell all the materials only for Pidyon Shevuyim. But if they have completed the building, they need not sell the synagogue, but must raise more money (for Pidyon Shevuyim) from the community. Mishneh Torah, Laws of Gifts to the Poor 8:11

❷

אין פודין את השבויים ביתר על דמיהן מפני תקון העולם, שלא יהיו האויבים רודפין אחריהם לשבותם, ואין מבריחין את השבויים מפני תקון העולם שלא יהיו האויבים מכבידין עליהן את העול ומרבים בשמירתן.

One should not pay an exorbitant amount of money in order to redeem captives. Paying too large a sum will encourage kidnappers to continue taking captives. One should not attempt to rescue captives because this will cause the captors to treat the captives worse, and to watch them more closely.

Mishneh Torah, Laws of Gifts to the Poor 8:12

❸

האשה קודמת לאיש להאכיל ולכסות ולהוציא מבית השבי, מפני שהאיש דרכו לחזר לא האשה ובושתה מרובה, ואם היו שניהם בשביה ונתבעו שניהן לדבר עבירה האיש קודם לפדות לפי שאין דרכו לכך.

A woman takes precedence over a man when both require food, clothing, and redemption from captivity because it is accepted for a man to go around begging, but not for a woman whose embarrassment is greater. If the two of them are in captivity and both are forced into a situation that might cause them to sin [commentaries on this passages generally believe the act to be sexual relations with a male], the man takes precedence to be redeemed because it is against his nature.

Mishneh Torah, Laws of Gifts to the Poor 8:15

❹

היו לפנינו עניים הרבה או שבויים הרבה ואין בכיס כדי לפרנס או כדי לכסות או כדי לפדות את כולן, מקדימין את הכהן ללוי, ולוי לישראל...

If there are many poor people or many captives but not enough money to support, clothe, or redeem them all, then a Kohen takes precedence over a Levi, and a Levi takes precedence over a Yisrael...

Mishneh Torah, Laws of Gifts to the Poor 8:17

❺

במה דברים אמורים בשהיו שניהן שוין בחכמה, אבל אם היה כהן גדול עם הארץ וממזר תלמיד חכם, תלמיד חכם קודם, וכל הגדול בחכמה קודם את חבירו, ואם היה אחד מהן רבו או אביו אע"פ שיש שם גדול מהן בחכמה, רבו או אביו שהוא תלמיד חכם קודם לזה שהוא גדול מהם בחכמה.

Under what conditions do these priorities take effect? When they are both equal in wisdom. However, if there was an ignorant Kohen Gadol (High Priest) and a scholarly mamzer [offspring of a marriage prohibited in the Torah], the scholar takes precedence. Whoever has the greater wisdom takes precedence over the other. If one of the captives is his teacher or his father, even though another captive has greater wisdom, his teacher or father who is learned takes precedence over the other, wiser captive. Mishneh Torah, Laws of Gifts for the Poor, 8:18

QUESTIONS FOR THOUGHT

- How have the concerns of the rabbis changed from the time that Horayot was written, until approximately 800 years later during the time of Maimonides?
- What historical conditions can you think of that might have effected these changes?
- What seems to be the basic reasoning or logic that underlies their priorities?
- Which of the rules, if any from the Talmud and according to Maimonides do you think would still be valid today?

➤ Can you think of a specific case and/or time that we previously mentioned in this chapter where these rules would apply?

➤ One of Judaism's most important principles is that every human life is of equal value. The Mishnah says that only one man was created in the beginning so that no person could say to another, "My father was greater than yours because we all have one common father (Sanhedrin chap.4, Mishna 5). If this is true, how can Jewish law say that one person takes precedence over another when it comes to redeeming captives?

IDENTIFYING PERSONAL PRIORITIES FOR PIDYON SHEVUYIM

EXERCISE: Who Should be Saved?

What characteristics or circumstances should be taken into account when deciding whom to save first?

I.____

2. ____

3. ____

4. ____

5. ____

6. ____

7. ____

TRADITION TESTS MAIMONIDES' THEORIES

Now read the two texts below. After you read them, go back and review your list. Might these two texts influence a change in your list?

א"ל רבינא לרב אשי: גבו זוזי ומחתי, מאי? אמר ליה: דילמא מיתרמי
להו פדיון שבויים ויהבי להו. שריגי ליבני והדרי הודרי ומחתי כשורי, מאי? א"ל:
זמנין דמתרמי להו פדיון שבויים, מזבני ויהבי להו. א"ה, אפי' בנו נמי! אמר ליה:
דירתיה דאינשי לא מזבני.

Ravina asked Rav Ashi: "Suppose money [for a synagogue] has been collected and is ready for use, is there still a risk?" He replied: "They may be called on to redeem captives and use it for that purpose." (Ravina asked further): "Suppose the bricks are already piled up and the lathes trimmed and the beams ready, what are we to say?" He replied: "It can happen that money is suddenly required for the redemption of captives, and they may sell the material for that purpose." "If they could do that", (he said), "they could do the same even if they had already built the synagogue!" He answered: "People do not sell their dwelling places." Baba Batra 3b

איפרא הורמיז אימיה דשבור מלכא, שדרה ארנקא דדינרי לקמיה דרב יוסף, אמרה: ליהוי
למצוה רבה. יתיב רב יוסף וקא מעיין בה, מאי מצוה רבה? א"ל אביי, מדתני רב
שמואל בר יהודה: אין פוסקין צדקה על היתומים אפילו לפדיון שבוים, שמע מינה:
פדיון שבוים מצוה רבה היא. אמר ליה רבא לרבה בר מרי: מנא הא מילתא
דאמור רבנן דפדיון שבוים מצוה רבה היא? א"ל, דכתיב: (ירמיהו טו) והיה
כי יאמרו אליך אנה נצא ואמרת אליהם כה אמר ה' אשר למות למות ואשר לחרב
לחרב ואשר לרעב לרעב ואשר לשבי לשבי, ואמר רבי יוחנן: כל המאוחר בפסוק
זה קשה מחבירו. חרב קשה ממות - אי בעית אימא: קרא, ואי בעית אימא:
סברא- אי בעית אימא סברא, האי קא מינוול והאי לא קא מינוול ואבע"א קרא
(תהלים קט"ז) יקר בעיני ה' המותה לחסידיו. רעב קשה מחרב - איבעית
אימא סברא, האי קא מצטער והאי לא קא מצטער איבעית אימא קרא.
(איכה ד') טובים היו חללי חרב מחללי רעב. שבי [קשה מכולם,] דכולהו איתנהו ביה.

Ifra Hormiz the mother of King Shapur sent a chest of gold coins to Rav Yosef, with the request that it should be used for carrying out some very important religious precept. R. Yosef was trying hard to think what such a precept could be, when Abaye said to him, "Since Rav Samuel b. Judah has laid down the law that money for charity is not to be levied from orphans even for the redemption of captives, we may conclude that the redemption of captives is a religious duty of great importance."

Rava asked Rabbah b. Mari: "From where is the maxim of the Rabbis derived that the redemption of captives is a religious duty of great importance?" –He replied: "From the verse 'And it shall come to pass if they ask you, "Where shall we go forth," then you shall tell them, "Thus said the Lord: Such as are for death, to death, and such as are for the sword, to the sword, and such as are for famine, to the famine, and such as are for captivity, to captivity"'(Jeremiah 15:2)." [Commenting on this] R. Yohanan said, "Each punishment mentioned in this verse is more severe than the one before. The sword is worse than death; this I can demonstrate either from Scripture, or, if you prefer, from observation. The proof from observation is that the sword deforms but death does not deform; the proof from Scripture is in the verse, 'Precious in the eyes of the Lord is the death of His faithful' (Tehillim 116:15). Famine is harder than the sword; this again can be demonstrated either by observation, the proof being that the one causes [prolonged] suffering but the other not, or, if you prefer, from the Scripture, from the verse, "They that be slain by the sword are better then they that be slain with hunger' (Eicha 4:9). Captivity is harder than all, because it includes the sufferings of all."
Baba Batra 8a-8b

Based on your personal lists, and on the lists that you made with regard to the Jewish texts, think about the following questions:

- How do your priorities agree or disagree with the guidelines given in the Talmud and the Mishneh Torah:
- Traditionally, the mitzvah of helping captives was called 'ransoming captives.' Why do you think Jews 'ransomed' captives?
- Could this mitzvah still be called 'ransoming captives' today? Why or why not? If you think a new name for this mitzvah is required, suggest one.
- Where should 'saving captives' fit into the other activities and necessities of life?
- How can you become more involved in this idea of Pidyon Shvuyim?

PUTTING PIDYON SHEVUYIM INTO PRACTICE: TAKING ACTION

You can play an active role in the world-wide effort to end the suffering and restore the freedom of the four Israeli soldiers Missing in Action through letter writing to government officials. In addition, you can increase public awareness by copying photos of the MIA's and hanging them on your synagogue's school bulletin boards, lobbies, and gift shops. Encourage the leadership of your congregation to launch its own campaign for the MIA's. Encourage your congregations to designate a special Shabbat as "Shabbat Ne'edarei Zahal"—a Sabbath to remember Israel's MIA's. An empty chair should be reserved on the bimah of the synagogue and on the dais during celebrations of Jewish life and freedom to remember that Israel's sons are still being held captive. Another great way to raise your community's awareness is to write a "letter-to-the-editor" in your synagogue's newsletter, as well as your community's newspaper.
American Zionist Movement MIA Action Fact Sheet

A Greater Understanding of Love Your Neighbor as Yourself

Redeeming the life of another can be one of the greatest mitzvot.

UNITED SYNAGOGUE YOUTH
TIKUN OLAM PROGRAM

DESCRIPTIONS OF TZEDAKOT

The organizations that follow represent only a portion of the agencies and Tzedakot that the International USY Tikun Olam Committee considered to receive allocations in 1999.

AGUDAH LEMA'AN HACHAYAL
Comparable to the USO in some respects, it provides special supplies and services to soldiers in Israel. It also offers recreational and educational activities to soldiers during times that would otherwise be most distressing.

AKIM
A voluntary association in Jerusalem and surrounding areas that provides assistance to mentally retarded and developmentally disabled adults whose old and ailing parents can no longer care for them at home. Akim provides educational, residential, and leisure time services for about 1000 persons, while always researching for new and creative models of service delivery.

ALYN
The Alyn Woldenberg Orthopedic Hospital and Rehabilitation Center for physically handicapped children in Israel treats patients up to 18 years of age, offering physiotherapy, occupational therapy and treatment, to psychologists and social workers. Alyn services 100 in-patients, 20 day patients and has a lengthy waiting list. In the past, our funds have been used for special trips, the out-patient clinic, music therapy programs, and new orthopedic appliances.

AMICHAI
Founded at the time of Operation Moses, AMICHAI serves as a Citizen's Advice Bureau for part of the Ethiopian Jewish community in Israel. Recognizing the cultural trauma with which they were faced, AMICHAI set out to raise a generation of young leaders who would feel at home in both the normative Jewish culture of Israel, and in their own traditions.

BEIT ZIPPORAH
In operation since 1981, Beit Zipporah is a shelter in Jerusalem for battered women and their children. They have been able to provide shelter for twenty people at a time. No matter how long each woman stays in the shelter, the fact that she has been there and has begun to break through the wall of secrecy and silence and shame gives her strength to face her future choices, and to make choices independently.

BIKUR CHOLIM GENERAL HOSPITAL
This Jerusalem hospital provides all modern medical needs, including new departments of Ophthalmology, Ear, Nose, and Throat, and General Surgery. These new departments are in addition to clinical laboratories and out-patient clinics. It is the only hospital in downtown Jerusalem. Our funds help buy specialized equipment needed by the hospital.

CHAI LIFELINE/ "CAMP SIMCHA"
Chai Lifeline is designed to help the Jewish patients and families of those dealing with cancer and other life-threatening diseases. The camp then others these children a chance to get away from home and feel/act like the children they are with specific care for their health needs, while offering their families a respite from caring for them. All programs are offered free of charge.

CHAZON F'TAYA
People from every mental institution in Jerusalem come to Chazon Fetaya to work in a bookbindery, sewing workshop and at other jobs. Some retarded and elderly people also work there. Their work is an important part of their rehabilitation.

CITIZENS COMMITTEE FOR PROTECTION OF JEWISH CEMETERIES AND CULTURAL MONUMENTS IN POLAND

This unique group works to protect, preserve, and, where possible, restore Jewish relics and monuments throughout Poland. Their work includes the restoration of cemeteries as well as synagogue restoration. They are also active in stimulating and supporting Jewish history and culture in Poland.

COMMITTEE FOR ETHIOPIAN JEWS IN SAFED

Over 750 Ethiopian Jews have now settled in the Safed area in Northern Israel. The Committee has been instrumental in the absorption and resettlement process. They provide for basic needs, such as winter clothing and also educational and recreational needs, such as computer equipment, new playgrounds, and summer camp scholarships.

COMMUNITY FOSTER CARE CENTERS

These homes, located in Jerusalem, provide a family atmosphere for children from problematic family situations. They maintain contact with their families but are able to live in a more healthy family environment most of the year.

DISCRETIONARY FUND

From time to time emergency situations arise which require immediate action, and cannot await the annual Allocations Committee Meeting. A limited amount of funds will be set aside each year to respond to these needs. Decisions as to the utilization of these funds will be made by the President of USY, the SATO Vice-President and SATO Committee Chairpeople.

DYSAUTONOMIA FOUNDATION

The foundation promotes research into a rare hereditary disease that afflicts only Ashkenazic Jews. The disease is a malfunction of the autonomic nervous system, which controls involuntary processes, such as swallowing, sucking, the opening of the tear ducts, and the awareness of the sensations of hot and cold. Money is needed to promote extensive research to prevent dysautonomia in unborn children. Twenty-five percent of all dysautonomic children die by the age of ten because of complications.

EZRAT NASHIM/SARAH HERZOG MEMORIAL HOSPITAL

Sarah Herzog is one of Israel's oldest social service organizations, maintaining the Jerusalem Mental Health Center. The center is a non-profit, private facility that treats and rehabilitates mentally ill men, women and children. It depends solely on private charitable contributions for its maintenance.

FOUNDATION FOR THE ADVANCEMENT OF YIDDISH STUDIES

This organization is dedicated to teaching and spreading knowledge of Yiddish language and culture in Israel and other parts of the world. Two of their important projects are providing Yiddish language classes in Israeli public schools (using new Russian olim as teachers) and sending Yiddish teachers to the former Soviet republics.

FUCHSBERG CENTER FOR CONSERVATIVE JUDAISM

The official Israeli address for the United Synagogue of Conservative Judaism. The center, which includes a synagogue, a yeshiva, conference space, and a youth hostel, as well as various offices, conducts many outreach programs in Jerusalem for all segments of the community. Over the years our contributions have been used for a broad variety of purposes, including outreach to college students, adult education, and their Tzedakah Fund.

GAN TAZPIT

A diagnostic Kindergarten for the developmentally disabled, there are currently 40 children between the ages of three and seven at Gan Tazpit. They are grouped in five classes and their progress is encouraged and recorded by a director, two speech therapists, five teachers, an occupational therapist, a play therapist, etc. These are all children with delayed development. As recently as ten years ago, they would have been classified as retarded, and thus doomed to a lifetime of institutional environment.

GESHER FOUNDATION

This organization attempts to bridge the gap between the religious and secular populations in Israel through retreats, study programs, lectures, etc. aimed at high school students.

HALACHA INSTITUTE
This is a school for learning disabled students located in Haifa. Our funds are going towards the purchase of educational computer equipment.

HEBREW IMMIGRANT AID SOCIETY (HIAS)
The Hebrew Immigrant Aid Society is a worldwide migration agency that rescues Jews from oppression in various countries and resettles them in places where they can live in dignity. Our funds provide a scholarship for a new Jewish immigrant to pursue college or vocational studies.

HEVRA PROGRAM
The Hevra Program was founded in 1995 by the Far West Region of USY in conjunction with Camp Ramah in California. Based on the Tikvah "Buddy Program" at Camp Ramah, the Hevrah Program brings together Jewish teens with special needs and active USYers. While the Tikvah Buddy Program takes place during the summer at camp, the Hevra Program is available year-round in an urban setting. The program also provides educational programs for the USYers about the special needs associated with having a disability.

HOLOCAUST DOCUMENTATION CENTER
This project, under the direction of Dr. Simon Wiesenthal, has succeeded in bringing many Nazi War Criminals to justice. It is independently funded, and based in Vienna, Austria.

ILAN (JERUSALEM)
The Israel Foundation for Handicapped Children takes care of over 10,000 persons afflicted with neuromuscular handicaps, including individuals with polio, etc. As the largest voluntary organization in Israel, ILAN gives medical, educational, vocational, welfare and social attention and treatment to patients. The Sabin Scholarship Fund provides fees and maintenance for 1950 Polio Epidemic victims. Our funds help to provide special programming for the people at one of the sheltered workshops in Jerusalem, as well as equipment for their new workshop.

ILAN (HAIFA)
Also affiliated with the National Ilan framework (described above), our funds to this branch of Ilan are being used to construct and equip a sports and rehabilitation center for handicapped children in Haifa and the Northern part of Israel.

ISRAEL ELWYN
Israel Elwyn (formerly Jerusalem Elwyn) is a non-profit organization that provides rehabilitation and training services to children and adults with disabilities, including persons with developmental disabilities, Cerebral Palsy, autism, and physical and sensory impairments. Programs include vocational rehabilitation and training, supported employment, community-based group homes, special education schools, preschool programs, medical and dental services and adult development centers. Israel Elwyn currently serves more than 780 individuals in four major locations, in both East and West Jerusalem.

ISRAEL FREE LOAN ASSOCIATION
This is an interest-free loan fund for new Soviet Immigrants to Israel. Examples of purposes for which loans are given include emergency and unanticipated expenses, health and dental treatment, school supplies, food, clothing, basic furniture and utensils, basic household repairs, interest on debts such as mortgage payments, extra hours of homemaker service for the ill and homebound, expenses for Jewish holidays, college tuition, day care and other basic needs. Maximum grants are up to $1,000 per family if enough funds are available. New loans are not considered until a prior loan is repaid. They strive not to duplicate government (national and municipal), Jewish Agency, or other tax-based services currently available to Russian Immigrants.

JAFFA INSTITUTE FOR THE ADVANCEMENT OF EDUCATION
Its programs range from youth clubs to bar mitzvah projects, and from audio-visual reading enhancement to field trips, and summer camps. Its work with the underprivileged is done in coordination with the existing schools and other local bodies to improve the quality of life for these young people.

JERUSALEM POST TOY FUND
This fund (in existence since 1950) provides toys at Chanukah time for needy children in Israel, and is sponsored by contributions to the Jerusalem Post from all over the world.

JEWISH BRAILLE INSTITUTE OF AMERICA
Centered in New York, the Jewish Braille Institute provides services for the Jewish Blind throughout North America. This includes religious training through tapes and transcription of Braille materials in Hebrew such as Siddurim and Chumashim. Our contributions have been used for the low vision center in Tel-Aviv, to expand the tape library in New York, to print a large-print edition of the Torah, and for programs in Eastern Europe

JEWISH DEAF CONGRESS, INC
This is the only organization which provides services and resources for the Jewish Deaf on a national scale. Our funds are being used to create a national registry of Jewish sign language interpreters to help the Jewish deaf nationwide.

THE JEWISH FOUNDATION FOR THE RIGHTEOUS
Many of the non-Jews who risked their lives to save Jews during the Holocaust are now destitute. The Foundation raises funds to provide monthly stipends to financially needy rescuers. Occasionally they provide emergency funds for medical expenses, burial or other situations.

JEWISH NATIONAL FUND (JNF)--HILL 16
Well known to many for the millions of trees they have planted in Israel, USY's special JNF project is the sponsorship of land reclamation at Hill 16, outside Jerusalem.

JEWISH PRISONER SERVICES INTERNATIONAL
The Coalition, is dedicated to serving the needs of Jews in prison. The Coalition's network of volunteers, chaplains, rabbis, attorneys, social workers, ex-offenders and others responds to requests from Jewish inmates. These include requests for Jewish religious and study materials, correspondence, visitation, Shabbat and holiday observance, formation of congregations behind prison walls, post-release and halfway houses, and help in situations where anti-Semitism makes incarceration an even more difficult experience.

JEWISH THEOLOGICAL SEMINARY LIBRARY
The library at the Jewish Theological Seminary contains one of the largest and most exhaustive collections of Hebraica and Judaica in the world, totaling over 260,000 volumes. It includes thousands of books, periodicals, rare books, and manuscripts, including material from the Cairo Geniza. Tikun Olam is funding an endowment to purchase books about Jewish Education.

JEWS FOR JUDAISM
Jews For Judaism was formed as a reaction to the growing Christian Missionary activity directed at the Jewish community in the early '80's. Today, Christian Missionary groups number well over 500, and spend over $100 million dollars per year in their efforts to convert Jews. Jews For Judaism reached thousands of Jews each year in communities around the world with information on cult and missionary groups. It is the only full-time, counter-missionary, counter-cult organization in North America.

KEREN GEETA
Founded in memory of the daughter of Dr. Pesach Schindler, director of the Center in Jerusalem, who died at age 38, the Keren Geeta fund is designed to support projects which reflect her ideals and with which she was involved in order to do Tikun Olam. At the present time the money is being used to help fund environmental education programs in schools

KEREN OR CENTER
This is the only Jewish residential institution in the world devoted exclusively to the care and rehabilitation of blind children and youth with multiple disabilities, many of whom have been abandoned by their parents because of their complicated needs.

KESHER
Established to fill the gap in the health care system for families with children with disabilities and chronic illnesses in Israel. Kesher provides information assistance, counseling and referrals, and is the only service designed specifically to help parents and families to cope better with everyday difficulties of raising their children.

KIBBUTZ HANATON
The first Conservative or Masorti Kibbutz in Israel. The settlement opened its doors to its first group of settlers in the Fall of 1984. It is located in the Galilee near Nazareth. USY alumni are amongst the first settlers. Tikun Olam funds have been used for Siddurim, Chumashim, Educational materials, furnishings for their synagogue and other equipment.

LIBI FUND
The LIBI Fund was set up in 1980 in order to assist the Israel Defense Forces (IDF) in financing essential projects relating to improving the quality of people and equipment in the force. Our funds are currently used to finance a special army preparation course for new immigrants.

LINDA FELDMAN RAPE CRISIS CENTER
The center provides immediate and follow-up services to victims of rape and sexual assault. It hopes to become the focus of statistical and treatment information about rape and rape victims in Jerusalem. Our funds have provided for various public awareness campaigns. As well as programs to help prevent teenage rape.

JERUSALEM COUNCIL FOR THE ELDERLY
The Council acts as an umbrella group for representatives of organizations dealing with the elderly throughout Jerusalem. It helps promote cooperation between these groups and raise public awareness for the needs of the elderly population. One of their major projects for which our funds have been utilized, is a program to install safety devices in the homes of elderly persons living alone so that they can continue to live independently with fewer risks. This year our money is funding a program called "Bridges Between Generations" which helps build relationships between high school students and the elderly in their communities through group programs and volunteer work.

LOS ANGELES JEWISH AIDS SERVICES
Their overall goals are to raise the community's awareness of AIDS as an issue in the Jewish Community and to provide support to Jewish people with AIDS and their families. They run various HIV/AIDS prevention programs within Jewish educational settings for both students and their parents. It is run through the Jewish Family Services division of the Los Angeles Jewish Federation (UJA).

MAGEN DAVID ADOM
As Israel's equivalent to the Red Cross, Magen David Adom has provided emergency medical aid wherever and whenever needed, through its 75 branches. It runs the only blood fractionation and processing plant in Israel, and provides concentrated training in first aid techniques and emergency treatment. Funds are used for supplies ranging from sterilized wound dressings to a fully-equipped ambulance and for the training of paramedics.

MASORTI MOVEMENT
The Masorti movement is the Israeli equivalent of the American Conservative movement. It sponsors USY's sister movement in Israel, Noar Masorti, the network of Tali schools which provide Masorti education within the Israel school system, and provides help for the many Masorti congregations in Israel. Our funds are being used for a bar/bat mitzvah program for new olim from the former Soviet Union.

MICHA (JERUSALEM)
Micha's programs work to enable the deaf child from early age to use his residual hearing and activate his sense of understanding and speech development and help him enjoy his childhood like other children. Our funds have helped to purchase books, toys, playground equipment, and hearing aids for the children.

MISHOLIM
The Jerusalem Expressive Therapy Center for Children. The center is run by a group of educators and therapists who have specialized in the treatment of children with emotional and organic problems. Such children have difficulty expressing themselves and establishing the Interpersonal relationships necessary for their normal development. Therefore, they need a special program in which use is made of creative and expressive methods as the means of treatment.

NATIONAL TAY SACHS ASSOCIATION
This non-profit, philanthropic organization was formed to raise funds for, and to promote research into Tay-Sachs and allied neurodegenerative diseases of infancy and childhood; to support and promote programs of carrier detection and prevention; and to assist the families of afflicted children by making available to them counseling facilities, out-patient clinics and the opportunity to participate in the purposes and programs of the association.

NATIONAL YIDDISH BOOK CENTER
The world's first and only organization devoted to saving Yiddish books and making them available to libraries, universities and scholars around the world. They have already collected hundreds of thousands of books and have saved them from destruction. They have distributed volumes to students scholars and libraries in twenty countries on five continents. Our funds are used for a scholarship for the summer intern program and their summer Yiddish camp program.

NEVE HANNA
This residential facility in Kiryat Gat cares for 50 children, most of whom come from broken homes and other problematic situations. Our funds are going to provide Chanukah presents for the residents, and to support their regular programs.

NEVE MENASHE PARENTS COMMITTEE
The Neve Menashe Home is a government owned institution in the Haifa area. There are 400 residents aged 3-56 years. Most of the residents are severely retarded and about 80 of them are also physically handicapped. They live in groups of 24 persons to a house. The home is now gradually being rebuilt by government funds as it is very old. Unfortunately the government does not provide more than the bare essentials. The parent's committee tries to help with items of equipment which, will make life more pleasant for their sons and daughters.

NORTH AMERICAN CONFERENCE ON ETHIOPIAN JEWRY
Founded in 1982 NACOEJ, is a grassroots, largely volunteer organization whose purpose has historically been to help Ethiopian Jews survive in Ethiopia, emigrate to Israel, and thrive in their new homeland while still preserving their unique culture. NACOEJ primarily facilitates absorption, education, and cultural preservation in Israel to both new and more experienced immigrants. Our funds currently go to a scholarship to sponsor an Ethiopian student who is studying at Haifa U.

PROJECT EZRA
Designed to work with Jewish aged and poor on New York's Lower East Side and based in a local synagogue, the program consists of providing companionship as well as physical assistance on a one-to one basis.

PROJECT VISION
This program, run by Dr. Stephen S. Kutner of Atlanta, Georgia, makes laser eye surgery available to low income patients in Israel. All services are provided at no charge. Funds from Tikun Olam go towards the purchase of needed equipment (e.g. Argon and YAG lasers) to set up clinics in Israel and worldwide.

RABANIT BRACHA KAPACH
The Rabanit (Rabbi's Wife) takes care of hundreds of people throughout the Nachalat Shiva neighborhood of Jerusalem, as well as other neighborhoods. She provides wedding dresses for brides who cannot afford their own, summer camping for kids and Shabbat provisions for poor families. Our funds are directed to her Passover food program which reaches more than 2,000 families.

RAMAH CHILE (SANTIAGO, CHILE JEWISH COMMUNITY)
This Jewish summer program for which we provide scholarships, is for members of the Beth El youth movement, which is affiliated with the Conservative Movement in South America. They work in conjunction with the Comunidad Israelita de Santiago and the Seminario Rabbinico Latinoamericano.

RAMBAM HOSPITAL
Located in Haifa, Rambam Hospital is close to Israel's Northern Command. One of the hospitals most important areas is their rehabilitation and physiotherapy program, to which our funds are applied.

REENA FOUNDATION
The Reena Foundation's ultimate goal is to maximize the potential of men and women who are developmentally handicapped in an effort to support them towards independent living within their communities. The program includes residential services, support groups, travel programs (including to Israel), and recreational activities.

SEMINARIO RABBINICO LATINOAMERICANO
The Rabbinical Seminary of Latin America and Communidad Beth El in Buenos Aires, Argentina, serve a large Jewish Community by supporting and expanding the program of translating into Spanish, printing, and distributing important Jewish works, and offering scholarships to South American Students for study at the Jewish Theological Seminary in New York (with the provision that the students will serve in South American for a specified period afterward). Our funds are helping them to set up a department of Yiddish culture to help protect the language and culture from extinction that was expedited by the Shoah.

SCHECHTER INSTITUTE OF JEWISH STUDIES
The first Conservative Rabbinical Seminary in Israel was founded in 1984 in order to provide leadership for the Masorti (Conservative) Movement there. The rabbis and educators who graduate from the Seminary will serve in Conservative Congregations in Israel and will provide leadership for Noar Masorti, USY's sister organization there.

SHAARE ZEDEK HOSPITAL
This institution in Jerusalem provides full hospital services to persons in every age group. A new hospital center was completed in 1978; It is the most modern health facility in Israel. Our contributions have been directed to the neo-natal intensive care unit, and for emergency care.

SHALVA
Shalva was officially opened in June 1990 in Israel. Shalva provides services for children with mental and physical disabilities, all of which are offered free of charge. Shalva works under the premise that children will thrive and develop more in a home situation than if they are institutionalized. Shalva provides support and assistance to parents so that they can cope with the challenges and pressures of bringing up a child with disabilities.

SHEKEL/PROGRAMS FOR SPECIAL NEEDS CHILDREN
This program creates educational and recreational programs for special needs children and children from dysfunctional homes in Jerusalem. Our funds are used to help sponsor a variety of their activities including building gardens for their respite program.

THE THERAPEUTIC RIDING CLUB OF ISRAEL
The Therapeutic Riding Club was established in 1986. Its purpose is to promote the recovery of disabled individuals through horseback riding, support related medical research and to train and certify therapeutic riding instructors. Therapeutic riding helps improve muscle tone, balance, posture, co-ordination, motor development and emotional and physical well-being.

TIKVAH PROGRAM OF CAMP RAMAH
The Tikvah Program is an exciting experiment in Jewish Education that offers a chance for "special" teens with learning programs to join the Jewish Community of Camp Ramah for the Summer. There, in an integrated setting, the campers participated in classes, swimming sports and in everything else available to the Ramah Camper. Where the Tikvah Campers have special needs, they receive special education; where they have strengths, they are given every opportunity to build on them. Tikvah programs exist at Ramah Camps in New England, Wisconsin, Canada, and California.

YAD BENJAMIN
A project for over 300 high school boys in Israel, including recent immigrants, the school provides agricultural training, technical training, and a health center. They also provide a Yeshiva program for boys whom for various reasons have not been accepted to established Yeshiva high schools. Children from the neighboring settlements in the Nahal Sorek District receive vocational training near their homes.

YAD EZRA
Yad Ezra helps the deprived and needy in Israel. It finds work for the mentally disturbed, provides interest-free food loans, constructs health clinics, established discount supermarkets, provides non-profit catering for weddings and b'nai mitzvah, and distributes free food parcels for Shabbat to impoverished families.

YAD L'KASHISH (LIFELINE FOR THE OLD)
In Jerusalem, this institution trains and employs hundreds of elderly and needy in its 12 workshops, giving the old a sense of pride and dignity. USY Pilgrimage visits this institution as part of their educational program. Our funds have been used for the dental clinic, for nutrition counselors with the Meals on Wheels Program, and for repairs to the facilities.

YAD LAYELED
This Educational Museum on the Child in the Holocaust is housed at the Ghetto Fighters' House, the museum of the Holocaust and Resistance in Israel's Galilee. The children's museum, including a memorial, helps children learn about the Holocaust through an experiential approach.

YAD SARAH
A voluntary organization in Israel, with centers throughout the country, Yad Sarah provides medial equipment on loan to all who require it, asking only a nominal fully refundable deposit. Yad Sarah centers are open round the clock to provide for emergencies.

ABOUT THE AUTHOR OF THE REVISED EDITION

Dara Zabb is a rabbinical student at the Jewish Theological Seminary of America. A former program director for the Washington Institute for Jewish Leadership and Values, Dara graduated from the University of Maryland and has worked for the Department of Youth Activities of the United Synagogue of Conservative Judaism in a number of educational capacities.